Character Building

Character Building

Booker T. Washington

MINT EDITIONS

Character Building was first published in 1902.

This edition published by Mint Editions 2020.

ISBN 9781513271132 | E-ISBN 9781513276137

Published by Mint Editions®

MINT
EDITIONS

minteditionbooks.com

Publishing Director: Jennifer Newens
Design & Production: Rachel Lopez Metzger
Project Manager: Micaela Clark
Typesetting: Westchester Publishing Services

Contents

Preface

A number of years ago, when the Tuskegee Normal and Industrial Institute was quite small, with only a few dozen students and two or three teachers, I began the practice of giving what were called Sunday Evening Talks to the students and teachers. These addresses were always delivered in a conversational tone and much in the same manner that I would speak to my own children around my fireside. As the institution gradually grew from year to year, friends suggested that these addresses ought to be preserved, and for that reason during the past few years they have been stenographically reported. For the purpose of this book they have been somewhat revised; and I am greatly indebted to my secretary, Mr. Emmett J. Scott, and to Mr. Max Bennett Thrasher, for assisting me in the revision and in putting them into proper shape for publication; and to Mr. T. Thomas Fortune for suggesting that these addresses be published in book form.

In these addresses I have attempted from week to week to speak straight to the hearts of our students and teachers and visitors concerning the problems and questions that confront them in their daily life here in the South. The most encouraging thing in connection with the making of these addresses has been the close attention which the students and teachers and visitors have always paid, and the hearty way in which they have spoken to me of the help that they have received from them.

During the past four years these addresses have been published in the school paper each week. This paper, *The Tuskegee Student*, has a wide circulation among our graduates and others in the South, so that in talking to our students on Sunday evening I have felt in a degree that I was speaking to a large proportion of the coloured people in the South. If there is anything in these addresses which will be of interest or service to a still wider audience, I shall feel I have been more than repaid for any effort that I have put forth in connection with them.

Booker T. Washington
Tuskegee, Alabama

Two Sides of Life

There are quite a number of divisions into which life can be divided, but for the purposes of this evening I am going to speak of two; the bright side of life and the dark side.

In thought, in talk, in action, I think you will find that you can separate life into these two divisions—the dark side and the bright side, the discouraging side and the encouraging side. You will find, too, that there are two classes of people, just as there are two divisions of the subject. There is one class that is schooling itself, and constantly training itself, to look upon the dark side of life; and there is another class, made up of people who are, consciously or unconsciously, constantly training themselves to look upon the bright side of life.

Now it is not wise to go too far in either direction. The person who schools himself to see the dark side of life is likely to make a mistake, and the person who schools himself to look only upon the bright side of life, forgetting all else, also is apt to make a mistake.

Notwithstanding this, I think I am right in saying that the persons who accomplish most in this world, those to whom on account of their helpfulness the world looks most for service—those who are most useful in every way—are those who are constantly seeing and appreciating the bright side as well as the dark side of life.

You will sometimes find two persons who get up in the morning, perhaps a morning that is overcast with shadows—a damp, wet, rainy, uninviting morning—and one of these persons will speak of the morning as being gloomy, will speak of the mud-puddles about the house, of the rain, and of all of the disagreeable features. The second person, the one who has schooled himself to see the brighter side of life, the beautiful things in life, will speak of the beauties that are in the rain drops, and the freshness of the newly bathed flowers, shrubs and trees. Notwithstanding the gloomy and generally disconsolate appearance of things, he will find something attractive in the scene out of doors, and will discover something in the gloomy morning that will cheer him.

Suppose that you see these same two persons eat their breakfast. Perhaps they will find out that the rolls are bad, but that the coffee is excellent. If the rolls are poor, it is a great deal better in such a case to get into the habit—a habit that you will find pays from every standpoint—of being able to forget how unpalatable they are, and to let your thoughts dwell upon the good and satisfactory coffee. Call the attention of your near neighbour at the table to the excellence of the coffee. What is the result of that kind of schooling? You will grow up to be an individual whom people will like to see coming near them—an individual to whom people will go for encouragement when the hours are dark, and when everything seems to be discouraging.

In just the same way, when you go into the class-rooms to recite your lessons, do not dwell upon any mistakes that you may think you see the teacher make, or upon any weakness in the presentation of the lesson. All teachers make mistakes sometimes, and you may depend upon it that it is an excellent teacher and a person of fine character who, when he or she has made a mistake, says frankly and plainly, "I have made a mistake," or "I don't know." It takes a very good and a very bright teacher to say, "I don't know." No teacher knows everything about every subject. A good teacher will say frankly and clearly, "I don't know. I cannot answer that question."

Let me tell you, right here, too, that when you go out from here to become teachers yourselves—as a large proportion of you will go—whenever you get to a point where a student asks you a question which you are not able to answer, or asks you something about a subject on which you are not well informed, you will find it better to say frankly and honestly, "I am unable to answer your question." Your students will respect you a great deal more for your frankness and honesty. Education is not what a person is able to hold in his head, so much as it is what a person is able to find. I believe it was Daniel Webster who said that the truly educated man was not the one who had all knowledge in his head, but the one who knew where to look for information upon any subject upon which at any time he might want information. Each individual who wishes to succeed must get that kind of discipline. He must get such training that he will know where to go and get facts, rather than try to train himself to hold all facts in his head.

I want you to go out from this institution so trained and so developed that you will be constantly looking for the bright, encouraging and beautiful things in life. It is the weak individual, as a rule, who is constantly calling attention to the other side—to the dark and discouraging things of life. When you go into your classrooms, I repeat, try to forget and overlook any weak points that you may think you see. Remember, and dwell upon, the consideration that has been given to the lesson, the faithfulness with which it was prepared, and the earnestness with which it is presented. Try to recall and to remember every good thing and every encouraging thing which has come under your observation, whether it has been in the class-room, or in the shop, or in the field. No matter where you are, seize hold on the encouraging things with which you come in contact.

In connection with the personality of their teachers, it is very unfortunate for students to form a habit of continually finding fault, of criticising, of seeing nothing but what the student may think are weak points. Try to get into a frame of mind where you will be constantly seeing and calling attention to the strong and beautiful things which you observe in the life and work of your teachers. Grow into the habit of talking about the bright side of life. When you meet a fellow student, a teacher, or anybody, or when you write letters home, get into the habit of calling attention to the bright things of life that you have seen, the things that are beautiful, the things that are charming. Just in proportion as you do this, you will find that you will not only influence yourself in the right direction, but that you will also influence others that way. It is a very bad habit to get into, that of being continually moody and discouraged, and of making the atmosphere uncomfortable for everybody who comes within ten feet of you. There are some people who are so constantly looking on the dark side of life that they cannot see anything but that side. Everything that comes from their mouths is unpleasant, about this thing and that thing, and they make the whole atmosphere around them unpleasant for themselves and for everybody with whom they come in contact. Such persons are surely undesirable. Why, I have seen people coming up the road who caused me to feel like wanting to cross over on to the other side of the way so as not to meet them. I didn't want to hear their tales of misery and woe. I had heard those tales so many times that I didn't want to get into the atmosphere of the people who told them.

It is often very easy to influence others in the wrong direction, and to grow into such a moody fault-finding disposition that one not only is miserable and unhappy himself, but makes every one with whom he comes in contact miserable and unhappy. The persons who live constantly in a fault-finding atmosphere, who see only the dark side of life, become negative characters. They are the people who never go forward. They never suggest a line of activity. They live simply on the negative side of life. Now, as students, you cannot afford to grow in that way. We want to send each one of you out from here, not as a negative force, but as a strong, positive, helpful force in the world. You will not accomplish the task which we expect of you if you go with a moody, discouraged, fault-finding disposition. To do the most that lies in you, you must go with a heart and head full of hope and faith in the world, believing that there is work for you to do, believing that you are the person to accomplish that work, and the one who is going to accomplish it.

In nine cases out of ten, the person who cultivates the habit of looking on the dark side of life is the little person, the miserable person, the one who is weak in mind, heart and purpose. On the other hand, the person who cultivates the habit of looking on the bright side of life, and who calls attention to the beautiful and encouraging things in life is, in nine cases out of ten, the strong individual, the one to whom the world goes for intelligent advice and support. I am trying to get you to see, as students, the best things in life. Do not be satisfied with second-hand or third-hand things in life. Do not be satisfied until you have put yourselves into that atmosphere where you can seize and hold on to the very highest and most beautiful things that can be got out of life.

HELPING OTHERS

T here are a few essential things in an institution of this kind that I think it is well for you to keep ever before you.

This institution does not exist for your education alone; it does not exist for your comfort and happiness altogether, although those things are important, and we keep them in mind; it exists that we may give you intelligence, skill of hand, and strength of mind and heart; and we help you in these ways that you, in turn, may help others. We help you that you may help somebody else, and if you do not do this, when you go out from here, then our work here has been in vain.

You would be surprised to know how small a part of your own expenses you pay here. You pay but little; and by reason of that fact it follows that as trustees of the funds which are given to this institution, we have no right to keep an individual here who we do not think is going to be able to go out and help somebody else. We have no right to keep a student here who we do not think is strong enough to go out and be of assistance to somebody else. We are here for the purpose of educating you, that you may become strong, intelligent and helpful.

If you were paying the cost of your board here, and for your tuition, and fuel and lights, then we should have a different problem. But so long as it is true that you pay so small a proportion of your expenses as you do, we must keep in view the fact that we have no right to keep a student here, no matter how much we may sympathize with him or her, unless that student is going to be able to do somebody else some good. Every young man and every young woman should feel that he or she is here on trust, that every day here is a sacred day, that it is a day that belongs to the race. Our graduates, and the majority of the students that have gone out from here, have ever had an unselfish spirit, and have been willing to go out and work at first for small salaries, and in uncomfortable places, where in a large degree conditions have been discouraging and desolate. We believe that kind of spirit will continue to exist in this institution, and that we shall continue to have students who will go out from here to make other persons strong and useful.

Now no individual can help another individual unless he himself is strong. You notice that the curriculum here goes along in three directions—along the line of labour, of academic training, and of moral and religious training. We expect those who are here to keep strong, and to make themselves efficient in these three directions, in each of which you are to learn to be leaders.

Some people are able to do a thing when they are directed to do it, but people of that kind are not worth very much. There are people in the world who never think, who never map out anything for themselves, who have to wait to be told what to do. People of that kind are not worth anything. They really ought to pay rent for the air they breath, for they only vitiate it. Now we do not want such people as those here. We want people who are going to think, people who are going to prepare themselves. I noticed an incident this morning. Did you ever hear that side door creak on its hinges before this morning? The janitor ought to have noticed that creaking and put some oil on the hinges without waiting to be told to do it. Then, again, this morning I noticed that after it had been raining hard for twenty-four hours, when it was wet and muddy, no provision had been made to protect the hogs at the sty, and they were completely covered with mud. Now the person who had charge of the sty should not have waited for some one to tell him to go down there and put some straw in for bedding and put boards over the sty to keep the animals dry. No one in charge of the hogs ought to have waited to be told to do a thing like that. The kind of persons we want here are those who are not going to wait for you to tell them to do such things, but who will think of them for themselves and do them. If we cannot turn out a man here who is capable of taking care of a pig sty, how can we expect him to take care of affairs of State?

Then, again, some of you are expected to take care of the roads. I should have liked to have seen boys this morning so much interested in working on the roads that they would have put sawdust from this building to the gate. I should have liked to see them put down some boards, and arrange for the water to drain off. We want such fellows as those here. The ones we want are the ones who are going to think of such things as these without being told. That is the only kind of people worth having. Those who have to wait to have somebody else put ideas into their minds are not worth much of anything. And, to be plain with you, we cannot have such people here. We want you to be thinkers, to be leaders.

Yesterday, and the night before, I travelled on the Mobile and Ohio railroad from St. Louis to Montgomery, and there was a young man on the same train who was not more than twenty years old, I believe, who recently had been appointed a special freight agent of the road. All his conversation was about freight. He talked freight to me and to everybody else. He would ask this man and that man if they had any freight, and if so he would tell them that they must have it shipped over the Mobile and Ohio railroad. Now that man will be general freight agent of that road some day: he may be president of the road. But suppose he had sat down and gone to sleep, and had waited for some one to come to him to inquire the best way to ship freight. Do you suppose he would ever have secured any freight to ship?

Begin to think. If you cannot learn to think, why, you will be of no use to yourself or anybody else. Every once in a while—about every three months—we have to go through the process of "weeding out" among the students. We are going to make that "weeding out" process more strict this year than ever before. We are compelled to get rid of every student here who is weak in mind, weak in morals, or weak in industry. We cannot keep a student here unless he counts for one. You must count one yourself. You eat for one, you drink for one, and you sleep for one; and so you will have to count for one if you are going to stay here.

I want you to go out into the world, not to have an easy time, but to make sacrifices, and to help somebody else. There are those who need your help and your sacrifice. You may be called upon to sacrifice a great deal; you may have to work for small salaries; you may have to teach school in uncomfortable buildings; you may have to work in desolate places, and the surroundings may be in every way discouraging. And when I speak of your going out into life, I do not confine you to the schoolroom. I believe that those who go out and become farmers, and leaders in other directions, as well as teachers, are to succeed.

The most interesting thing connected with this institution is the magnificent record that our graduates are making. As the institution grows larger, we do not want to lose the spirit of self-sacrifice, the spirit of usefulness which the graduates and the students who have gone out from here have shown. We want you to help somebody else. We want you not to think of yourselves alone. The more you do to make somebody else happy, the more happiness will you receive in turn. If you want to be happy, if you want to live a contented life, if you want to live a life of genuine pleasure, do something for somebody else. When you feel unhappy, disagreeable and miserable, go to some one else who is miserable and do that person an act of kindness, and you will find that you will be made happy. The miserable persons in this world are the ones whose hearts are narrow and hard; the happy ones are those who have great big hearts. Such persons are always happy.

Some of the Rocks Ahead

I feel sure that I can be of some degree of service to you to-night, in helping you to anticipate some of the troubles that you are going to meet during the coming year. "Do not look for trouble," is a safe maxim to follow, but it is equally safe to prepare for trouble.

All of you realize, of course, that where we have so large a machine as we happen to have here—when I speak of machine in this way you will understand that I refer to the school—it takes some time to get it into perfect order, or anything bordering upon perfect running order. Now, I repeat, it is the wise individual who prepares himself beforehand for the day of difficulties, for the day of discouragements, for the rainy day. It is the wise individual who makes up his mind that life is not going to be all sunshine, that all is not going to be perpetual pleasure. What is true of everyday life is true of school life; there are a number of difficulties which it is probable you are going to meet or which are going to meet you during the coming school year, and which, if possible, I want you to prepare yourselves against as wisely as you can.

In the first place, a great many of you are going to be disappointed—if this has not already been the case—in the classes to which you will be assigned. The average individual thinks he knows a great deal more than he does know. The individual who really knows more than he thinks he knows is very rare indeed. When a student gets to the point where he knows more than he thinks he knows, that student is about ready to leave school. I wish a very large number of you had reached that point. I repeat, numbers of you are going to be disappointed during the year as to the classes to which you are going to be assigned.

Now, I want to give you this advice. Before you go to an institution examine the catalogue of that school. The catalogue will give you all the information about the school. Then make up your mind whether or not you have faith in that institution. Find out if it is the school you wish to attend, and then decide if you have faith enough in it to become its pupil. Then, if you have once done this, make up your mind that those who are placed over you as your teachers have had more experience than you can have had, and that they are therefore able to advise you as to your classes. Make up your mind that if you are asked to go into a lower class than you think your ability entitles you to go into, you are going to follow the advice and instruction of the people who are older than you and who have more education than you have.

Another way in which you are going to be disappointed, and be made homesick, perhaps, if you have not already been made so, is in the rooms to which you are going to be assigned. You are going to get rooms that you do not like. They will not be, perhaps, as attractive as you desire, or they will be too crowded. You are going to be given persons for room mates with whom you think it is going to be impossible to get along pleasantly, people who are not congenial to you. During the hot months your rooms are going to be too hot, and during the cold months they are going to be too cold. You are going to meet with all these difficulties in your rooms. Make up your mind that you are going to conquer them. I have often said that the students who in the early years of this school had such hard times with their rooms have succeeded grandly. Many of you now live in palaces, compared to the rooms which those students had. I am sure that the students who attend this school find that the institution is better fitted every year to take care of them than it was the year previous. From year to year there has been a steady growth in the accommodations, and that is all that we can wish or expect. From year to year we do not forget that it is our duty to make students more comfortable than in previous years, and we are steadily growing, in that direction. But notwithstanding all this we cannot do all that we want to do.

Make up your minds, then, that you are going to find difficulties in your room, in reference to your room mates, the heat, the cold, and any number of things that concern your stay in the buildings. But in all these matters keep in mind the high purpose for which you came here—to get an education. Get that thought into your heart and body, and it will enable you to be the master of all these little things, all these minor and temporary obstacles.

Many of you are going to be disappointed in regard to your food. Notwithstanding all the care we may try to take, and want to take, many of you are going to be disappointed in this respect. But how little is the meaning of one meal, how little a thing is being inconvenienced by one meal, as compared with something that is going to be a part of you all the remainder of your lives. It is not for the food, the room, or the minor things that you have come here; it is to get something into your minds and hearts that will make you better, that will stand by you and hold you up, and make you useful all through life.

Some of you are going to find it difficult to obey orders. Sometimes orders will be given you which you think are wrong and unjust. Perhaps orders will be given you sometimes that really are unjust. In that respect no institution is perfect. But I want you to learn this lesson in respect to orders—that it is always best to learn to obey orders and respect authority—that it is better ten times over for you to obey an order that you know is wrong, and which perhaps was given you in a wrong spirit or with a mistaken motive. It is better for you to obey even such an order as that, than it is for any individual to get into the habit of disobeying and not respecting those in authority.

Make up your mind that if you want to add to your happiness and strength of character, you are, before all things else, going to learn to obey. If it should happen that for a minute, or five minutes, one of your fellow-students is placed in authority over you, that student's commands should be sacred. You should obey his commands just as quickly as you would obey those of the highest officer in this institution. Learn that it is no disgrace to obey those in authority. One of the highest and surest signs of civilization is that a people have learned to obey the commands of those who are placed over them. I want to add here that it is to the credit of this institution that, with very few exceptions, the students have always been ready and willing to respect authority.

I want you to see, as I think you will see, that having a hard time, running up against difficulties here and there, helps to make an individual strong, helps to make him powerful. This is the point I want to make with you; that one of the reasons you are here is that you may learn to overcome difficulties. I have named some that you may expect to meet, but I have not named them all. They will keep springing up all the time. Just in proportion as you learn to rise above them and trample them under your feet, just in that proportion will you accomplish the high purpose for which you came here, and help to accomplish the purpose for which this institution exists.

On Influencing by Example

A few evenings ago, while in Cincinnati, I was very pleasantly surprised after speaking at a large meeting to be invited by a company of young coloured men to attend for a few minutes a reception at their club room. I expected, when I went to the place designated, to find a number of young men who, perhaps, had hired a room and fitted it up for the purpose of gratifying their own selfish pleasures. I found that this was not the case. Instead, I found fifteen young men whose ages ranged from eighteen to twenty years, who had banded themselves together in a club known as the "Winona Club," for the purpose of improving themselves, and further, for the purpose, so far as possible, of getting hold of other young coloured men in the city who were inclined in the wrong direction. I found a room beautifully fitted up, with a carpet on the floor, with beautiful pictures upon the walls, with books and pictures in their little library, and with fifteen of the brightest, most honest, and cleanest looking young men that it has been my pleasure to meet for a long time.

It was a very pleasant surprise to find these young men, especially in the midst of the temptations of a Northern city, in the midst of evil surroundings, banded together for influencing others in the right direction.

These young men came together, and at their first meeting said that they were going to band themselves together for the purpose of improving themselves and helping others. They said that the first article in their constitution should be to the effect that there should be no gambling in that club; that there must be no strong drink allowed in that club, and that there should be nothing there that was not in keeping with the life of a true and high-minded gentleman.

I repeat that it was very pleasant and encouraging for me to find such work as this going on in Cincinnati. What was equally gratifying, and surprising, was that at the close of the reception they presented me with a neat sum of money which they had collected, and asked that this money be used to defray the expenses of some student at the school here.

Now the point I especially want to make to-night is this: all of you must bear in mind the fact that you are not only to keep yourselves clean, and pure, and sober, and true, in every respect, but you owe a constant responsibility to yourself to see that you exert a helpful influence on others also.

A large proportion of you are to go from here into great cities. Some of you will go into such cities as Montgomery, and some, perhaps, will go into the cities of the North—although I hope that the most of you will see your way clear to remain in the South. I believe that you will do better to remain in the country districts than to go into the cities. I believe that you will find it to your advantage in every way to try to live in a small town, or in a country district, rather than in a city. I believe that we are at our best in country life—in agricultural life—and too often at our worst in city life. Now when you go out into the world for yourselves, you must remember in the first place that you cannot hold yourselves up unless you keep engaged and out of idleness. No idle person is ever safe, whether he be rich or poor. Make up your minds, whether you are to live in the city or in the country, that you are going to be constantly employed.

In a rich and prosperous country like America there is absolutely no excuse for persons living in idleness. I have little patience with persons who go around whining that they cannot find anything to do. Especially is this true in the South. Where the soil is cheap there is little or no excuse for any man or woman going about complaining that he or she cannot find work. You cannot set proper examples unless you, yourself, are constantly employed. See to it, then, whether you live in a city, a town, or in a country district, that you are constantly employed when you are not engaged in the proper kind of recreation, or in rest. Unless you do this you will find that you will go down as thousands of our young men have gone down—as thousands of our young men are constantly going down—who yield to the temptations which beset them.

Refrain from staking your earnings upon games of chance. See to it that you pass by those things which tend to your degradation. Teach this to others. Teach those with whom you come in contact that they cannot lead strong, moral lives unless they keep away from the gambling table. See to it that you regulate your life properly; that you regulate your hours of sleep. Have the proper kinds of recreation. Quite a number of our young men in the cities stay up until twelve, one and two o'clock each night. Sometimes they are at a dance, and sometimes at the gambling table, or in some brothel, or drinking in some saloon. As a result they go late to their work, and in a short time you hear them complaining about having lost their positions. They will tell you that they have lost their jobs on account of race prejudice, or because their former employers are not going to hire coloured help any longer. But you will find, if you learn the real circumstances, that it is much more likely they have lost their jobs because they were not punctual, or on account of carelessness.

Then, too, you will find that you will go down if you yield to the temptation of indulging in strong drink. That is a thing that is carrying a great many of our young men down. I do not say that all of our men are of this class, or that all of them yield to temptations, because I can go into many of the large cities and find just such men as those in Cincinnati to whom I have referred. You cannot hope to succeed if you keep bad company. As far as possible try to form the habit of spending your nights at home. There is nothing worse for a young man or young woman than to get into the habit of thinking that he or she must spend every night on the street or in some public place.

I want you, as you go out from this institution, whether you are graduates or not, whether you have been here one year or four years—to go out with the idea that you must set a high example for every one in your community. You must remember that the people are watching you every day. If you yield to the temptation of strong drink, of going into bad company, others will do the same thing. They will shape their lives after yours. You must so shape your lives that the hundreds and thousands of those who are looking to you for guidance may profit by your example.

The Virtue of Simplicity

I hope that you all paid strict attention to what Mr. William H. Baldwin, Jr., who recently spoke to you, had to say. In the few words that he spoke, I think he told you the platform upon which this institution has been built. You will remember that he laid a great deal of stress upon the importance of the institution remaining simple, of keeping that degree of simplicity and thoroughness that it has always possessed.

It is true that in the last few months the institution has come into a great deal of prominence, and is meeting with what the world calls "success." But we must remember that very often it is with institutions as it is with individuals—success may injure them more than poverty. Now, this institution will continue to succeed, will continue to have the good will and confidence, the co-operation of the best and wisest and most generous people in the country, just so long as its faculty, its students, and all connected with it, remain simple, earnest and thorough. Just as soon as in any department there are indications that we are beginning to become what the world calls "stuck up," just so soon will the people lose confidence in us, and will fail to support us, and just so soon will the institution begin to decay. We will grow in buildings, in industries, in apparatus, in the number of teachers and of students, and in the confidence of the people, just in proportion as we do what the institution has set out to do; that is, teach young men and women how to live simple, plain and honourable lives by learning how to do something uncommonly well.

When I speak of humbleness and simplicity, I do not mean that it is necessary for us to lose sight of what the world calls manhood and womanhood; that it is necessary to be cringing and unmanly; but you will find, in the long run, that the people who have the greatest influence in the world are the humble and simple ones.

Now, we must not only remain humble, but we must be very sure that whatever is done in every department of the school is thoroughly done. Any institution runs a great risk when it begins to grow—to grow larger in numbers or larger in any respect. It can succeed then only in proportion as those who have responsibilities are conscientious in the highest degree. We can succeed in putting up good buildings only in proportion as every one performs well his part in the erection of each building. We can succeed only in proportion as the student who makes the mortar, who lays the bricks, puts his whole conscience into that work, and does it just as thoroughly as it is possible for him to do it. If he is mixing mortar, he must do it just as well as he can, and then, to-morrow, must do it still better than he did it to-day, and the next week better than he did it this week. The student who lays the bricks must learn to lay each brick as well as it is possible for him to lay it, and then do still better work on the morrow.

We must remember, too, that we have a certain amount of responsibility to care for our buildings, and that a great deal of interest should be taken not only in putting up all our buildings thoroughly, but in looking out for their preservation as well. We must see to it that the buildings which the students have worked so hard to erect, and which generous friends have so kindly enabled us to secure, are not marred in any way. You must make new students know that this property is yours, and that every building here is yours. No student has any right to mar in any way what you have worked so hard to erect, and your friends have been generous enough to provide. If you find a student drawing a lead pencil across a piece of plastering which you have put on, you must let that student know that he is destroying what you have worked hard to create, and that when he destroys that building he is destroying something which students yet to come should have the opportunity of enjoying.

We want to be sure that in every industry, in every department of the institution, there is simplicity, humbleness, thoroughness. Whatever is intrusted to you to do in the industrial departments, in the class rooms, be sure that you put your whole heart into that thing.

We do not expect to have fine, costly buildings, nor do we want to have them. But we do expect to have well-constructed buildings, and attractive buildings; and, if we can go on in this simple, humble way, the time will come when we shall have all the buildings we need. Just in proportion as our friends see that we are worthy of these good things, they will come to us.

We want to be sure, also, that in no department is there any wastefulness. We must try to make every dollar go as far as possible. "We must stretch a dollar," as I have heard Mr. Baldwin say, "until it can be stretched no further." Now, there will be waste unless we put our conscience into everything that we do. There will be waste in the boarding department, in the academic department, in the industrial department, in the religious department, in all the departments about us, unless we put our conscience into everything that we do. Let us be sure that not a single dollar that is given to us is wasted, because the same people who give to us are called upon almost every day in the week, each year, to give for hundreds of purposes, and they have to choose which they will support. They must decide whether they want to give to this cause, or to that cause, and they will give to us if we make them feel that we are more worthy than other similar institutions.

We want, also, to be sure that we remain simple in our dress and in all our outward appearance. I do not like to see a young man who is poor, and whose tuition is being paid by some one, and who has no books, sometimes has no socks, sometimes has no decent shoes, wearing a white, stiff, shining collar which he has sent away to be laundered. I do not like to ask people to give money for such a young man as that. It is much better for a young man to learn to launder his collars himself, than to pretend to the world that he is what he is not. When you send a collar to the city laundry, it indicates that you have a bank account; it indicates that you have money ahead, and can afford that luxury. Now I do not believe that you can afford it; and that kind of pretence and that kind of acting do not pay.

Get right down to business, and, as I have said, if we cannot do up your collars well enough here to suit you, why, get some soap and water, and starch, and an iron, and learn to launder your own collars, and keep on laundering them until you can do them better than anybody else.

I am not trying to discourage you about wearing nice collars. I like to see every collar shine. I like to see every collar as bright as possible. I like to see you wear good, attractive collars. I do not, however, want you to get the idea that collars make the man. You quite often see fine cuffs and collars, when there is no real man there. You want to be sure to get the man first. Be sure that the man is there, and if he is, the collars and the cuffs will come in due time. If there is no man there, we may put on all the collars and cuffs we can get, and we shall find that they will not make the man.

When you have finished school, after you have gone out and established yourselves in some kind of business, after you have learned to save money, and have got a good bank account ahead, if you are where the laundering is not sufficiently well done to suit you, why perhaps you can afford to send your collars forty or fifty miles away. But as I see you young men, I do not believe you can afford it. And if you can afford it, why, I should like to have you pay that money for a part of your tuition, which we now have to get some one else to pay for you.

You want to be very sure, too, that as you go out into the world, you go out not ashamed to work; not ashamed to put in practice what you have learned here. As I come in contact with our graduates, I am very glad to be able to say that in almost no instance have I found a student who has been at Tuskegee long enough to learn the ways of the institution, or a graduate who has been ashamed to use his hands. Now that reputation we want to keep up. We want to be sure that such a reputation as this follows every student who goes out.

And then be very sure that you are simple in your words and your language. Write your letters in the simplest and plainest manner possible. Who of you did not understand what was said by Mr. John D. Rockefeller, Jr., when he spoke from this platform a few evenings ago? Was there a single word, or a single reference, or figure of speech, that he used that you did not understand the full force of, or did not appreciate? Here is a man whose father is perhaps the richest man in the world, and yet there was no "tomfoolery" about his speech. Every word was simple and plain, and everybody could understand everything that he said. He used no Latin or Greek quotations.

Some people get the idea that if they can get a little education, and a little money ahead, and can talk so that no one can understand them, they are educated. That is a great mistake, because nobody understands them, and they do not understand themselves. Now, the world has no sympathy with that kind of thing. If you have anything to write, write it in the plainest manner possible. Use just as few words as possible, and as simple words as possible. If you can get a word with one syllable that will express your meaning, use it in preference to one of two syllables. If you can not get a suitable word of one syllable, try to get one of two syllables instead of three or four. At any rate make your words just as short as possible, and your sentences as short and simple as you can make them. There is great power in simplicity, simplicity of speech, simplicity of life in every form. The world has no patience with people who are superficial, who are trying to show off, who are trying to be what the world knows they are not.

You know you sometimes get frightened and discouraged about the laws that some of the States are inclined to pass, and that some of them are passing, but there is no State, there is no municipality, there is no power on earth, that can neutralize the influence of a high, pure, simple and useful life. Every individual who learns to live such a life will find an opportunity to make his influence felt.

No one can in any way permanently hold back a race of people who are getting those elements of strength which the world recognizes, which the world has always recognized, and which it always will recognize, as indicating the highest type of manhood and womanhood. There is nothing, then, to be discouraged about. We are going forward, and we shall keep going forward if we do not let these difficulties which sometimes occur discourage us. You will find that every man and every woman who is worthy to be respected and praised and recognized will be respected and praised and recognized.

HAVE YOU DONE YOUR BEST?

(This talk was given at the middle of the school year)

I f you have not already done so—and I hope you have—I think that you will find this a convenient season for each one of you to stop and to consider your school-year very carefully; to consider your life in school from every point of view; to place yourselves, as it were, in the presence of your parents, or your friends at home; to place yourselves in the presence of those who stand by and support this institution; to place yourselves in the presence of your teachers and of all who are in any way interested in you.

Now, suppose you were to-night sitting down by your parents' side, by their fireside, looking them in the face, or by the side of your nearest and dearest friends, those who have done the most for you, those who have stood by you most closely. Suppose you were in that position. I want to ask you to answer this question, In considering your school life—in your studies, for example—during the year, thus far, have you done your best?

Have you been really honest with your parents, who have struggled, who have sacrificed, who have toiled for years, in ways you do not know of, in order that you might come here, and in order that you might remain here? Have you really been interested in them? Have you really been honest with your teachers? Have you been honest with those who support this institution? Have you really, in a word, in the preparation and recitation of your lessons, done your level best? Right out from your hearts, have you done your best? I fear that a great many of you, when you look your conscience squarely in the face, when you get right down to your real selves, at the bottom of your lives, must answer that you have not done your best. There have been precious minutes, there have been precious hours, that you have completely thrown away, hours for which you cannot show a single return.

Now, if you have not done your level best, right out straight from your heart, in the preparation and recitation of your lessons, and in all your work, it is not too late for you to make amends. I should be very sorry if I waited until the end of the term to remind you of this, because it would then be too late. There would be many of you with long faces, who would say, if you were reminded then, that you could have done so much better, would have been so much more honest with your parents and friends, if you had only been reminded earlier; and that in every way you would have made your lives so different from what they had been. Now, it isn't too late.

Grant, as I know that numbers of you will grant, that you have thrown away precious time, that you have been indifferent to the advice of your teachers, that you really haven't been honest with yourselves in the preparation of your lessons, that you have been careless in your recitations. I want you to be really honest with yourselves and say, from to-night on, "I am going to take charge of myself. I am not going to drift in this respect. I am going to row up the stream; and my life, as a schoolboy or a schoolgirl, is going to be different from what it has been."

Now place yourselves again in the presence of your parents, of those who are dearest to you, and answer this question, In your work, in your industrial work here, have you done your real best? In the field and in the shop, with the plough, the trowel, the hammer, the saw, have you done your level best? Have you done your best in the sewing room and in the cooking classes? Have you justified your parents in the sacrifice of time and money which they have made in order to allow you to come here? If you haven't done your best in these respects—and many of you haven't—there is still time for you to become a different man or woman. It isn't too late. You can turn yourselves completely around. Those of you who have been indifferent and slow, those of you who have been thoughtless and slovenly, those of you who have tried to find out how little effort of body or mind you could put into your industrial work here,—it isn't too late for you to turn yourselves completely around in that respect, and to say that from to-night you are going to be a different man or woman.

Have you done your level best in making your surroundings what the school requires, what your school life should be, in learning how to take care of your bodies, in learning how to keep your bodies clean and pure, in the conscientious, systematic use of the tooth brush? Have you done your best? Have you been downright honest in that respect, alone? Have you used the tooth brush just because you felt it was a requirement of the school, or because you felt that you could not be clean or honest with your room-mates, that you could not be yourself in the sight of God, unless you used the tooth brush? Have you used it in the dark, as well as in the light? Have you learned that, even if your room was not going to be inspected on a certain day, it was just as important that you learn the lesson of being conscientious about keeping it in order as if you knew it was going to be inspected? Have you been careful in this respect? Have you shifted this duty, or neglected that duty? Have you thrown some task off on to your room-mates? Have you tried to "slide out" of it, or, as it were, "to get by," as the slang phrase goes, without doing really honest, straightforward work, as regards the cleanliness of your room, the improvement of it, the making of it more attractive?

Have you been really honest with yourselves and your parents, and with those who spend so much money for the support of this institution? Above all, have you been really true to your parents and to your best selves in growing in strength of character, in strength of purpose, in being downright honest? Those of you who came here, for instance, with the habit of telling falsehoods, of deceiving in one way or another; those of you who came here with the temptation, perhaps, in too many cases, overshadowing you and overpowering you, to take property which does not belong to you; have you been really honest in overcoming habits of this kind? Are you building character? Are you less willing to yield to temptation? Are you more able to overcome temptation now than you were? If you are not more able, you have not grown in this respect.

But it is not too late. If there are some of you who have been unfortunate enough to allow little mean habits, mean dispositions, mean acts, mean thoughts, mean words, to get the uppermost of you— in a word, if your life thus far has been a little, dried-up, narrow life, get rid of that life. Throw open your heart. Say now, "I am not going to be conquered by little, mean thoughts, words and acts any longer. Hereafter all my thoughts, all my words, all my acts, shall be large, generous, high, pure."

In a word, I want you to get hold of this idea, that you can make the future of your lives just what you want to make it. You can make it bright, happy, useful, if you learn this fundamental lesson, and stick to it while in school, or after you go away from here, that it doesn't pay any individual to do any less than his very best. It doesn't pay to be anything else but downright honest in heart. Any person who is not honest, who is not trying to do his very best in the classroom or in the shop, no matter where he may be, will find out that it does not pay in the long run. You may think it best for a little while, but permanently it does not pay any man or woman to be anything but really, downright honest, and to do his or her level best.

BOOKER T. WASHINGTON

Now I want you to think about these things, not only here in the chapel to-night, but to-morrow in your class-rooms, and with reference to everything you touch. I want to see you let it shine out, even at the very ends of your fingers, that you are doing your best in everything. Do this, and you will find at the end of the year that you are growing stronger, purer, and brighter, that you are making your parents and those interested in you happier, and that you are preparing yourselves to do what this institution and the country expect you to do.

Don't be Discouraged

Last Sunday evening I spoke to you for a few minutes regarding the importance of determining to do the right thing in every phase of your school life. There are a few things that enter into student life which, in a very large degree, cause the untrue to fall by the wayside, and which prevent students from doing their very best. Among these things is the disposition to grow discouraged. Very many people, very many students, who otherwise would succeed, who would go through school creditably, graduating with honours, have failed to succeed because they became discouraged.

Now there are a number of things in school life that cause a student to become discouraged, and I am going to try to enumerate a few of them, although I do not know that I shall mention nearly all of them.

Students frequently become discouraged on account of their industrial work. It is not of the character that they want it to be, or they do not get assigned to the trade they want to work at. Still others become discouraged because of their classroom studies. They find that their studies are difficult; that their lessons are too long and their memories too short. They find that they cannot understand the teacher, or they think they find that the teacher does not understand them. Some become discouraged because they think that they are entirely misunderstood, are misunderstood by their classmates and by their teachers. They think that their efforts in the classroom and in the shop are not properly appreciated.

Others become discouraged because they feel that they are without friends. It seems to them that other students have friends on every hand who are encouraging them, who send them money, who supply them with clothing, and that they themselves have no such friends.

You become discouraged for such reasons as these. You feel that your highest and best efforts are not appreciated. This tends to discourage you. There are not a few of you who get discouraged because you feel that you belong to a despised race; that for a long time you have been trampled upon because of your colour, and because of certain peculiar characteristics; that you have been neglected or oppressed, and that there is no reason why you should make an effort to go forward; that you belong to a race that is doomed to disappointment, to stay under, and to not succeed.

Some of you become discouraged and despondent because of poverty. Perhaps here I strike the basis of the reason for most of the discouragement. You come here, and your parents disappoint you. They do not supply you with money. You become discouraged because they do not supply you with proper clothing, or with what you think you ought to have, and, very often, with such as you really ought to have, and that disheartens you. You find that other students have money, and you have none. They have money not only for the necessities of school life, but for some of the luxuries, while you have not enough for even the bare necessities. Other students are more than supplied with clothing, while you are very scantily supplied. You shiver, in many cases, by reason of the cold, while others are comfortable and nicely dressed. Sometimes you are even ashamed to show yourself in public, because of the appearance of the old coat, or trousers, or shoes that you have to wear.

Some of you become discouraged because you find yourselves without the proper books. Some of you cannot get the money needed to purchase books, a tooth brush, and other necessary things. You find yourselves cramped and hampered on every hand. You are discouraged at this point and at that point, and you feel that nobody's lot is as hard as your own. You become discouraged, you become dissatisfied, and you feel like giving up.

Now I want to suggest to you to-night that this very thing of discouragement, as an element in life, is for a purpose. I do not believe that anything, any element of your lives, is put into them without a purpose. I believe that every effort that we are obliged to make to overcome obstacles will give us strength, will give us a confidence in ourselves, that nothing else can give us. I would ten times rather see you having a hard struggle to elevate yourselves, having a hard time either at work on the farm, or on the buildings, or in the shops, without money and without clothes, than to see you here having too much money, and having everything that you want come to you without any effort on your part. You are blessed, as compared with some people. The man or woman who has money, without having had to work for it, who has all the comforts of life, without effort, and who saves his own soul and perhaps the soul of somebody else, such an individual is rare, very rare indeed.

Now it is not a curse to be situated as some of you are, and if you will make up your minds that you are going to overcome the obstacles and the difficulties by which you are surrounded, you will find that in every effort you make to overcome these difficulties you are growing in strength and confidence. Make up your minds that you are not going to allow anything to discourage you. Make up your minds that poor lessons, scoldings on the part of your teachers, want of money, want of books—that none of these shall discourage you. Make up your mind that in spite of race and colour, in spite of the obstacles that surround you, in spite of everything, you are going to succeed in your school life, and are going to prepare yourself for usefulness hereafter.

Every person who has grown to any degree of usefulness, every person who has grown to distinction, almost without exception has been a person who has risen by overcoming obstacles, by removing difficulties, by resolving that when he met discouragements he would not give up. Make up your minds that you are going to overcome every discouragement, and that you are not going to let any discouragement overcome you. Those of you who have been inclined to be moody and morose, or have been inclined to feel that the whole world is against you, that there is no use for you to try to elevate yourselves, make up your minds that your future is just as bright as that of anybody else. Do this, and you will find that you have it in your own power to make your future bright or gloomy, just as you desire.

On Getting a Home

Every coloured man owes it to himself, and to his children as well, to secure a home just as soon as possible. No matter how small the plot of ground may be, or how humble the dwelling placed on it, something that can be called a home should be secured without delay.

A home can be secured much easier than many imagine. A small amount of money saved from week to week, or from month to month, and carefully invested in a piece of land, will soon secure a site upon which to build a comfortable house. No individual should feel satisfied until he has a comfortable home. More and more the Southern States are making one of the conditions for voting, the ownership of at least $300 worth of property, so that persons who own homes will not only reap the benefits that come from owning a home, in other directions, but will also find themselves entitled to cast their ballot.

Care should be taken as to the location of the land. It is of little advantage to secure a lot in some crowded, filthy alley. One should try to secure a lot on a good street, a street that is carefully and well worked, so that the surroundings of the home will be enjoyable. Even if one has to go a good ways into the country to secure such a lot, it is much better than to buy a building spot on an unsightly, undesirable alley.

I believe that our people do best, as a rule, to buy land in the country instead of in the city; but in either case we should not rest until we have secured a home in one place or the other. No man has a right to marry and run the risk of leaving his wife at his death without a home.

I notice with regret that there are many of our people who have already bought homes, who, after they have secured the land, paid for it and built a cabin containing two or three rooms, do not seek to go any further in the improvement of the property. In the first place, in too many cases, the house and yard, especially the yard, are not kept clean. The fences are not kept in repair. Whitewash and paint are not used as they should be. After the house is paid for, the greatest care should be exercised to see that it is kept in first-class repair; that the walls of the house and the fences are kept neatly painted or whitewashed; that no palings are allowed to fall off the fence, or if they do fall off, to remain off. If there is a barn or a henhouse, these should be kept in repair, and should, like the house, be made to look neat and attractive by paint and whitewash.

Paint and whitewash add a great deal to the value of a house. If persons would learn to use even a part of the time they spend in idle gossip or in standing about on the streets, in whitewashing or painting their houses, it would make a great difference in the appearance of the buildings, as well as add to their value.

Only a short time ago, near a certain town, I visited the house—I could not call it a home—of a presiding elder, a man who had received considerable education, and who spent his time in going about over his district preaching to hundreds and thousands of coloured people; and yet the home of this man was almost a disgrace to him and to his race. The house was not painted or whitewashed; the fence was in the same condition; the yard was full of weeds; there were no walks laid out in the yard; there were no flowers in it. In fact everything on the outside of the house and in the yard presented a most dismal and discouraging appearance. So far as I could see there was not a single vegetable around this house, nor did I see any chickens or fowls of any kind.

This is not the way to live, and especially is it not the way for a minister or a teacher to live, for they are men who are supposed to lead their people not only by word but by example. Every minister and every teacher should make his home, his yard, and his garden, models for the people whom he attempts to teach and lead. I confess that I have no confidence in the preaching of a minister whose home is in the condition of the one I have described. There is no need why, as a race, we should get into the miserable and unfortunate habit of living in houses that are out of repair, that are not whitewashed or painted, that are not comfortable, and above all else, in houses that we do not own. There is no reason why we should not make our homes not only comfortable, but attractive, so that no one can tell from the outside appearance, at least, whether the house is occupied by a white family or a black family.

. After a house has been paid for, it not only should be improved from year to year and kept in good repair, but, as the family grows, new rooms should be added. The house should not only be made comfortable, but should be made convenient. As soon as possible there should be a sitting room, where books and papers can be found, a room in which the whole family may read and study during the winter nights. I do not believe that any house is complete without a bathroom. As soon as possible every one of our houses should be provided with a bathroom, so that the body of every member of the family can be baptized every

BOOKER T. WASHINGTON

morning in clean, invigorating, fresh water. Such a bath puts one in proper condition for the work of the day, and not only keeps one well physically, but strong morally and religiously.

Another important part of the home is the dining-room. The dining-room should be the most attractive and most comfortable room in the house. It should be large and airy, a room into which plenty of sunlight can come, and a room that can be kept comfortable both in the summer and in the winter.

These suggestions are made to you with the hope that you will put them into practice, and also that you will influence others to do the same. They are all suggestions that we, as a race, notwithstanding our poverty, in most cases can find a way to put into practice. Every one of them should be taken up by our teachers, our ministers and by our educated young people. They should be taught and urged in school, in church, in farmers' meetings, in women's meetings, and, in fact, wherever the people of the race come together.

CALLING THINGS BY THEIR RIGHT NAMES

A few evenings ago I talked with you about the importance of learning to be simple, humble and child-like before going out into the world. You should remain in school until you get to the point where you feel that you do not know anything, where you feel that you are willing to learn from any one who can teach you.

Unfortunately there are many things here in the South which tend to lead away from this simplicity to which I have referred. There is a great inclination to make things appear what they are not. For example: take the schools. There is a great tendency to call schools by names which do not belong to them, and which do not correctly represent that which in reality exists. You will find the habit growing more prevalent every year, I fear, of calling a school a university, or a college, or an academy, or a high-school. In fact we seldom hear of a plain, common, public or graded school.

We do ourselves no good when we yield to that temptation. If a school is a public school, call it one; but do not think that we gain anything by calling a little country school, with two or three rooms and one or two teachers, where some of the students are studying the alphabet, a university. And still this is too often done throughout the South, as you know. No respect or confidence is gained by the practice, but, on the contrary, sensible people get disgusted with such false pretences. When you go out into the world and meet with such cases as this, try to make the people see that it is a great deal better to call their small public school by a name which truly represents it, than to call it a high-school or an academy. I do not by any means intend to say that schools do not have the right to aspire to become high-schools and colleges. What I mean to say is that it is hurtful to the race to get into the habit of calling every little institution of learning that is opened, a college or a university. It weakens us and prevents us from getting a solid, sure foundation.

Again, we make the same mistake when we call every preacher or person who stands in a pulpit to read from it, "Doctor," whether or not that degree has been conferred upon him. Sensible people get tired of that kind of thing. The degree of Doctor of Divinity was once held in the highest esteem, and was conferred only upon those ministers who had really become entitled to it because of some original research or other work of high scholarship. Among highly educated people this rule holds still. But to-day, especially in the South, many a little institution that opens its doors and calls itself a college or a university, is beginning to confer degrees, and make doctors of divinity of persons who are unworthy of degrees. And sometimes, should these persons fail to get an institution to confer a degree on them, they confer it on themselves! The habit is getting to be so common that in little towns the ministers are calling themselves Doctors. One pastor will meet another and say, "Good morning, Doctor," and the other, wishing to be as polite as his friend, will say, "How are you, Doctor?" and so it goes on, until both begin to believe they really are Doctors. Now this practice is not only ridiculous, but it is very hurtful to us as a race, and it should be discouraged.

Much the same criticism may be made of many of those who teach. A person who teaches a little country school, perhaps in a brush arbour, is called "Professor." Every person who leads a string band is called "Professor." I was in a small town not long ago, and I heard the people speaking of some one as "the professor." I was anxious to know who the professor was. So I waited a few minutes, and finally the professor came up, and I recognized him as a member of one of our preparatory classes. Now, don't suffer the world to put you in this silly, ridiculous position. If people attempt to call you "Professor," or by any other title that is not yours, tell them that you are not a professor, that you are a simple mister. That is a good enough title for any one. We have the same right to become professors as any other people, when we occupy positions which entitle us to that name, but we drag that title, which ought to be a badge of scholarship, down into the mud and mire when we allow it to be misapplied.

We carry a similar kind of deception into our school work when, in the essays which we read and the orations which we deliver, we simply rehearse matter a great deal of which has been copied from some one else. Go into almost any church where there is one of the doctors of divinity to whom I have referred, and you will hear sermons copied out of books and pamphlets. The essays, the orations, the sermons that are not the productions of the people who pretend to write them, all come from this false foundation.

Then there is another error to which I wish to call your attention. In many parts of the South, especially in the cities and towns, there are excellent public schools, well equipped in every way with apparatus and material, and provided with good, competent teachers, but in some cases these schools are crippled by reason of the fact that there are little denominational schools which deprive the public schools of their rightful attendance. If the school can't be in the church of some particular denomination, it must be near it. In the average town there may be the denominational school of the African Methodist Episcopal church, of the Zion church, of the Baptist church, of the Wesleyan Methodist church, and so on, all in different parts of the town. Instead of supporting one public school, provided at the expense of the town or city, there exists this little, narrow denominational spirit, which is robbing these innocent children of their education. We want to say to such people as these, people who are content so to deprive their children, and have them taught by some second-rate teacher, that they are wrong. We want you to let the people know that the great public-school system of America is the nation's greatest glory, and that we do not help matters when we attempt to tear down the public school. Of course it is the right and the duty of every denomination to erect its own theological seminaries and its colleges, where the special tenets of that denomination are taught to those who are preparing for its pulpit; but no one has a right to let this denominational spirit defeat the work of a public school to which all should be free to go.

I have in mind a place where the coloured people have an excellent school, equal to that of the whites. I went through the building and found it supplied with improved apparatus and capable teachers, and saw that first-class work was done there. Later, I was taken about a mile outside the city, where there was a school with an incapable teacher, and some sixty or seventy pupils being poorly taught. Here was a third-rate teacher in a third-rate building, poor work, and the children suffering for lack of proper instruction. Why? Simply because the people wanted a school of their own denomination in that part of the city.

Now you want to cultivate courage, and see to it that you are brave enough to condemn these wrongs and to show the people the mistakes which they make in these matters.

I mention all these things because they hinder us from getting a solid foundation. They hinder us, further, in that in many cases they prevent us from getting the right power of leadership in teaching, in the work of the ministry, and in many other respects. Wherever you go, then, make up your minds that you are going to make your influence felt in favour of better prepared teachers and preachers—in better preparation of all those who stand for leaders of the people. Just in proportion as you set your lives right in this matter, will the masses of the race be inclined to follow you.

European Impressions

Some people here in America think that some of us make too much ado over the matter of industrial training for the Negro. I wish some of the skeptics might go to Europe and see what races that are years ahead of us are doing there in that respect. I shall not take the time here to outline what is being done for men in the direction of industrial training in Europe, but I shall give some account of what I saw being done for women in England.

Mrs. Washington and I visited the Agricultural College for women, at Swanley, England, where we found forty intelligent, cultivated women, who were most of them graduates from high schools and colleges, engaged in studying practical agriculture, horticulture, dairying and poultry raising. We found the women in the laboratory and classrooms, studying agricultural chemistry, botany, zoölogy, and applied mathematics, and we also saw these same women in the garden, planting vegetables, trimming rose bushes, scattering manure, growing grapes and raising fruit in the hot-houses and in the field.

As another suggestion for our people, I might mention that while I was in England I knew of one of the leading members of Parliament leaving his duties in that body for three days to preside at a meeting of the National Association of Poultry Raisers, which was largely attended by people from all parts of the United Kingdom.

In the trip which Mrs. Washington and I made through Holland, we saw much which may be of interest to you. It has been said that, God made the world, but the Dutch made Holland. For one to fully realize the force of this one must see Holland for himself. One of the best ways to see the interior of Holland, and the peasant life, is to take a trip, as we did, on one of the canal boats plying between Antwerp, in Belgium, and Rotterdam, in Holland.

It was especially interesting for me to compare the rural life in Holland with the life of the country coloured people in the South. Holland has been made what it is very largely by the unique system of dykes or levees which have been built there to keep out the water of the ocean, and thus enable the people to use to advantage all the land there is in that small country.

The great lesson which our coloured farmers can learn from the Dutch, is how to make a living from a small plot of ground well

BOOKER T. WASHINGTON

cultivated, instead of from forty or fifty acres poorly tilled. I have seen a whole family making a comfortable living by cultivating two acres of land there, while our Southern farmers, in too many cases, try to till fifty or a hundred acres, and find themselves in debt at the end of the year. In all Holland, I do not think one can find a hundred acres of waste land; every foot of land is covered with grass, vegetables, grain or fruit trees. Another advantage which our Southern farmers might have in trying to pattern after the farmers of Holland, would be that they would not be obliged to go to so much additional expense for horse or mule power. Most of the cultivating of the soil there is done with a hoe and spade.

I saw the people of Holland on Sunday and on week days, but I did not see a single Dutch man, woman or child in rags. There were practically no beggars and no very poor people. They owe their prosperity, too, very largely to their thorough and intelligent cultivation of the soil.

Next to the thorough tilling of the soil, the thing of most interest there, from which the coloured people in America may learn a lesson, is the fine dairying which has made Holland famous throughout the world. Even the poorest family has its herd of Holstein cattle, and they are the finest specimens of cattle that it has ever been my pleasure to see. To watch thousands of these cattle grazing on the fields is worth a trip to Holland. As the result of the attention which they have given to breeding Holstein cattle, Dutch butter and cheese are in demand all through Europe. The most ordinary farmer there has a cash income as the result of the sale of his butter and milk.

Many of these people make more out of the wind that blows over the fields than our poor Southern people make out of the soil. The old-fashioned windmill is to be seen on every farm. This mill not only pumps the water for the live stock, but, in many cases, is made to operate the dairy, to saw the wood, to grind the grain, and to run the heavy machinery. These people are, however, not unlike our Southern people in one respect, and that is in having their women and children work in the fields. This, I think, is done in a larger measure even than in the South among the coloured people.

An element of strength in the farming and dairying interests of these people is to be found in the fact that many of the farmers have received a college or university training. After this they take a special course in agriculture and dairying. This is as it should be. Our people in the South will prosper in proportion as a larger number of university men take up agriculture and kindred callings after they have finished their academic education.

In the matter of physical appearance, including grace, beauty, and carriage of the body, I think our own people are far ahead of the Dutch. But the Dutch are a hardy, rugged, industrious race of people. In our trip in the canal boat we saw the men at the landings in large numbers, in their wooden shoes, and the women and children in their beautiful, old-fashioned head-dresses, each community having its own style of head-dress, which has been handed down from one generation to another.

We were in Rotterdam over Sunday. The free and rather boisterous commingling of the sexes on the street was noteworthy. In this, also, our people in the United States could set an example to the Dutch.

The foundation of the civilization of these people is in their regard for and respect for the law, and their observance of it. This is the great lesson which the entire South must learn before it can hope to receive the respect and confidence of the world. Europeans do not understand how the South can disregard its own laws as it so often does. If you ask any man on that side of the Atlantic why he does not emigrate to the Southern part of the United States, he shrugs his shoulders and says, "No law; they kill." I pray God that no part of our country may much longer have such a reputation as that in any part of the world.

From Holland we went to Paris. On a beautiful, sunny day, if you could combine the whirl of fashion and gaiety of New York City, Boston and Chicago on a prominent avenue, you would have some idea of what is to be seen in Paris upon one of her popular boulevards. Fashion seemed to sway everything in that great city; for example, when I went into a shoe store to purchase a pair of shoes, I could not find a pair large enough to be comfortable. I was gently told that it was not the fashion to wear large shoes there.

One of the things I had in mind when I went to France was to visit the tomb of Toussaint L'Ouverture, but I learned from some Haitian gentlemen residing in Paris that the grave of that general was in the northern part of France, and these same gentlemen informed me that his burial place is still without a monument of any kind. It seems that it has been in the minds of the Haitians for some time to remove his body to Haiti, but thus far it has been neglected. The Haitian Government and people owe it to themselves, it appears to me, to see to it that the resting place of this great hero is given a proper memorial, either in France or on the island of Haiti.

Speaking of the Haitians, there are a good many well educated and cultivated men and women of that nationality in Paris. Numbers of them are sent there each year for education, and they take high rank in scholarship. It is greatly to be regretted, however, that some of these do not take advantage of the excellent training which is given there in the colleges of physical science, agriculture, mechanics and domestic science. They would then be in a position to return home and assist in developing the agricultural and mineral resources of their native land. Haiti will never be what it should be until a large number of the natives receive an education which will enable them to develop agriculture, build roads, start manufactories, build railroads and bridges, and thus keep on the island the large amount of money which is now being sent outside for productions which these people themselves could supply.

In all the European cities which we visited, we compared the conduct of the rank and file of the people on the streets and in other places with that of our own people in the United States, and we have no hesitation in saying that, in all that marks a lady or gentleman, our people in the South do not suffer at all by the comparison. Even at the camp-meetings and other holiday gatherings in the South, the deportment of the masses of the coloured people is quite up to the standard of that of the average European in the larger cities which we saw.

I should strongly advise our people against going to Europe, and especially to Paris, with the hope of securing employment, unless fortified by strong friends and a good supply of money. In one week, in Paris, three men of my race called to see me, and in each case I found the man to be practically in a starving condition. They were well-meaning, industrious men, who had gone there with the idea that life was easy and work sure; but notwithstanding the fact that they walked the streets for days, they could get no work. The fact that they did not speak the language, nor understand the customs of the people, made their life just so much the harder. With the assistance of other Americans, I secured passage for one of these men to America. His parting word to me was, "The United States is good enough for me in the future."

The Value of System in Home Life

Most of you are going out from Tuskegee sooner or later to exert your influence in the home life of our people. You are going to have influence in homes of your own, you are going to have influence in the homes of your mothers and fathers, or in the homes of your relatives. You are going to exert an influence for good or for evil in the homes wherever you may go. Now the question how to bring about the greatest amount of happiness in these homes is one that should concern every student here. I say this because I want you to realize that each one of you is to go out from here to exert an influence. You are to exercise this influence in the communities where you go; and if you fail to exercise it for the good of other individuals, you have failed to accomplish the purpose for which this institution exists.

In the first place you want to exert your influence in those directions that will bring about the best results; among these it is important that the people have presented to them the highest forms of home life.

Very often I find it true—and especially the more I travel about among our people—that many persons have the idea that they cannot have comfortable homes unless they have a great amount of money. Now some of the happiest and most comfortable homes I have ever been in have been homes where the people have but little money; in fact, they might well be called poor people. But in these homes there was a certain degree of order and convenience which made you feel as comfortable as if you were in the homes of people of great wealth.

I want to speak plainly. In the first place there must be promptness in connection with everything in the life of the home. Take the matter of the meals, for instance. It is impossible for a home to be properly conducted unless there is a certain time for each meal, and promptness must be insisted on. In some homes the breakfast may be eaten at six o'clock one morning, at eight o'clock the next morning, and, perhaps, at nine o'clock the morning after that. Dinner may be served at twelve, one, or two o'clock, and supper may be eaten at five, six or seven; and even then one-half the members of the family be absent when the meal is served. There is useless waste of time and energy in this, and an unnecessary amount of worry. It saves time, and it saves a great amount of worry, to have it understood that there is to be a certain time for each meal, and that all the members of the family are to be present at that time. In this way the family will get rid of a great deal of annoyance, and precious time will be saved to be used in reading or in some other useful occupation.

Then as to the matter of system. No matter how cheap your homes are, no matter how poverty-stricken you may be in regard to money, it is possible for each home to have its affairs properly systematized. I wonder how many housekeepers can go into their homes on the darkest night there is, and put their hands on the box of matches without difficulty. That is one way to test a good housekeeper. If she cannot do this, then there is a waste of time. It saves time and it saves worry, too, if you have a certain place in which the matches are to be kept, and if you teach all the members of the family that the matches are always to be kept in that place. Oftentimes you find the match box on the table, or on a shelf in the corner of the room, or perhaps on the floor; sometimes here, sometimes there. In many homes five or ten minutes are wasted every day just on account of the negligence of the housekeeper or the wife in this little matter.

Then as to the matter of the dish cloth. You should have a place for your dish cloth, and put it there every day. The persons who do not have a place for an article are the persons who are found looking in-doors and out-of-doors for it, from five to ten minutes every time that article is needed. They will be saying, "Johnnie," or "Jennie, where is it? Where did you put it the last time you had it?" and all that kind of thing.

The same thing is true of the broom. In the first place, in the home where there is system, you do not find the broom left standing on the wrong end. I hope all of you know which the right end of the broom is in this respect. You do not find the broom on the wrong end, and you always find that there is a certain place for it, and that it is kept there. When things are out of place and you have to hunt for them, you are spending not only time, but you are spending strength that should be used in some more profitable way. There should be a place for the coat and the cloak, for the hat, and, in fact, a place for everything in the house.

The people who have a place for everything are the people who will find time to read, and who will have time for recreation. You wonder sometimes how the people in New England can afford to have so much time for reading books and newspapers, and still have sufficient money to send as much as they do here to this institute to be used in our education. These people find time to keep themselves thus intelligent, and to keep themselves in touch with all that takes place in the world, because everything is so well systematized about their homes that they save the time which you and I spend in worrying about something which we should know all about.

I have very rarely gone into a boarding house kept by our people and found the lamp in its proper place. When you go into such a house it is too apt to be the case that the people there will have to look for the lamp; then, when they have found it, it is not filled; somebody forgot to put the oil in it in the morning; then they have to go and hunt up a wick, and then they must get a chimney. Then, when they get all these things, they must hunt for the matches to light the lamp.

I wonder how many girls there are here now who can go into a room and arrange it properly for an individual to sleep in—that is, provide the proper number of towels, the soap and matches, and have everything that should be provided for the comfort of the person who is to use the room, put in the room and put in its proper place. I should be afraid to test some of you. You must learn to be able to do such things before you leave here, in order that you may be of some use to yourself and to others. If you are not able to do this, you will be a disappointment to us.

What Will Pay?

I wish to talk with you for a few minutes upon a subject that is much discussed, especially by young people—What things pay in life? There is no question, perhaps, which is asked oftener by a person entering upon a career than this—What will pay? Will this course of action, or that, pay? Will it pay to enter into this business or that business? What will pay?

Let us see if we can answer that question, a question which every student in this school should ask himself or herself. What will profit me most? What will make my life most useful? What will bring about the greatest degree of happiness? What will pay best?

Not long ago a certain minister secured the testimony of forty men who had been successful in business, persons who beyond question had been pronounced to be business men of authority. The question which this minister put to these business men was, whether under any circumstances it paid to be dishonest in business; whether they had found, in all their business career, that under any circumstances it paid to cheat, swindle or take advantage of their fellow-men, or in any way to deceive those with whom they came in contact. Every one of the forty answered, without hesitation, that nothing short of downright honesty and fair dealing ever paid in any business. They said that no one could succeed permanently in business who was not honest in dealing with his fellow-men, to say nothing of the future life or of doing right for right's sake.

It does not pay an individual to do anything except what his conscience will approve of every day, and every hour and minute in the day.

I want you to put that question to yourselves to-night: ask yourselves what course of action will pay.

You may be tempted to go astray in the matter of money. Think, when you are tempted to do that: "Will it pay?" Persons who are likely to go astray in the matter of money, furthermore are likely to do so in the matter of dress, in tampering with each other's property, in the matter of acting dishonestly with each other's books. Such persons will be dishonest in the matter of labour, too.

It pays an individual to be honest with another person's money. It never pays to be dishonest in taking another person's clothes or books.

None of these things ever pays, and when you have occasion to yield or not to yield to such a temptation, you should ask yourself the question: "Will it pay me to do this?" Put that question constantly to yourself.

Whenever you promise, moreover, to do a piece of work for a man, there is a contract binding you to do an honest day's labour—and the man to pay you for an honest day's labour. If you fail to give such service, if you break that contract, you will find that such a course of action never pays. It will never pay you to deal dishonestly with an individual, or to permit dishonest dealing. If you fail to give a full honest day's work, if you know that you have done only three-quarters of a day's work, or four-fifths, it may seem to you at the time that it has paid, but in the long run you lose by it.

I regret to say that we sometimes have occasion to meet students here who are inclined to be dishonest. Such students come to Mr. Palmer or to me, and say they wish to go home. When they are asked why they wish to go home, some of them say they wish to go because they are sick. Then, when they have been talked with a few minutes, they may say that they do not like the food here, or perhaps that some disappointment has befallen their parents. In some cases I have had students give me half a dozen excuses in little more than the same number of minutes.

The proper thing for students to do, when they wish to go home, is to state the exact reason, and then stick to it. The student who does that is the kind that will succeed in the world. The students who are downright dishonest in what they say, will find out that they are not strong in anything, that they are not what they ought to be. The time will come when that sort of thing will carry them down instead of up.

In a certain year—I think it was 1857—there was a great financial panic in the United States, especially in the city of New York. A great many of the principal banks in the country failed, and others were in daily danger of failure. I remember a story that was told of one of the bank presidents of that time, William Taylor, I believe. All the bank presidents in the city of New York were having meetings every night to find out how well they were succeeding in keeping their institutions solvent. At one of these meetings, after a critical day in the most trying period of the panic, when some men reported that they had lost money during that day, and others that so much money had been withdrawn from their banks during the day that if there were another like it they did not see how they could stand the strain, William Taylor reported that money had been added to the deposits of his bank that day instead of being withdrawn.

What was behind all this? William Taylor had learned in early life that it did not pay to be dishonest, but that it paid to be honest with all his depositors and with all persons who did business with his bank. When other people were failing in all parts of the country, the evidence of this man's character, his regard for truth and honest dealing, caused money to come into his bank when it was being withdrawn from others.

Character is a power. If you want to be powerful in the world, if you want to be strong, influential and useful, you can be so in no better way than by having strong character; but you cannot have a strong character if you yield to the temptations about which I have been speaking.

Some one asked, some time ago, what it was that gave such a power to the sermons of the late Dr. John Hall. In the usual sense he was not a powerful speaker; but everything he said carried conviction with it. The explanation was that the character of the man was behind the sermon. You may go out and make great speeches, you may write books or addresses which are great literature, but unless you have character behind what you say and write, it will amount to nothing; it will all go to the winds.

I leave this question with you, then. When you are tempted to do what your conscience tells you is not right, ask yourself: "Will it pay me to do this thing which I know is not right?" Go to the penitentiary. Ask the people there who have failed, who have made mistakes, why they are there, and in every case they will tell you that they are there because they yielded to temptation, because they did not ask themselves the question: "Will it pay?"

Go ask those people who have no care for life, who have thrown away their virtue, as it were, ask them why they are without character, and the answer will be, in so many words, that they sought but temporary success. In order to find some short road to success, in order to have momentary happiness, they yielded to temptation. We want to feel that in every student who goes out from here there is a character which can be depended upon in the night as well as in the day. That is the kind of young men and young women we wish to send out from here. Whenever you are tempted to yield a hair's breadth in the direction which I have indicated, ask yourself the question over and over again: "Will it pay me in this world? Will it pay me in the world to come?"

Education that Educates[1]

Perhaps I am safe in saying that during the last ten days you have not given much systematic effort to book study in the usual sense. When interruptions come such as we have just had, taking you away from your regular routine work and study, and the preparation of routine lessons is interrupted, the first thought to some may be that this time is lost, in so far as it relates to education in the ordinary sense; that it is so much time taken away from that part of one's life that should be devoted to acquiring education. I suppose that during the last few days the questions have come to many of you: "What are we gaining? What are we getting from the irregularity that has characterized the school grounds within the last week, that will in any degree compensate for the amount of book study that we have lost?"

To my mind I do not believe that you have lost anything by the interruption. On the other hand, I am convinced that you have got the best kind of education. I do not mean to say that we can depend upon it for all time to come for systematic training of the mind, but so far as real education, so far as development of the mind and heart and body are concerned, I do not believe that a single student has lost anything by the irregularity of the last week or more.

You have gained in this respect: in preparing for the reception and entertainment of the President of the United States and his Cabinet, and the distinguished persons who accompanied the party, you have had to do an amount of original thinking which you, perhaps, have never had to do before in your lives. You have been compelled to think; you have been compelled to put more than your bodily strength into what you have been doing. You could not have made the magnificent exhibition of our work which you have made if you had not been compelled to do original thinking and execution. Most of you never saw such an exhibition before; I never did. Those of you who had to construct floats that would illustrate our agricultural work and our mechanical and academic work, had to put a certain amount of original thought into the planning of these floats, in order to make them show the work to the best advantage; and two-thirds of you—yes, practically

---

1. This talk was given soon after the visit of President McKinley to Tuskegee Institute in the fall of 1898.

all of you—had never seen anything of the kind before. For this reason it was a matter that had to be thought out by you and planned out by you, and then put into visible shape.

Now compare that kind of education with the mere committing to memory of certain rules, or something which some one else thought out and executed a thousand years ago perhaps—and that is what a large part of our education really is. Education in the usual sense of the word is the mere committing to memory of something which has been known before us. Now during the last ten days we have had to solve problems of our own, not problems and puzzles that some one else originated for us. I do not believe that there is a person connected with the institution who is not stronger in mind, who is not more self-confident and self-reliant, so far as the qualities relate to what he is able to do with his mind or his hands, than he was ten or twelve days ago. There is the benefit that came to all of us. It put us to thinking and planning; it brought us in to contact with things that are out of the ordinary; and there is no education that surpasses this. I see more and more every year that the world is to be brought to the study of men and of things, rather than to the study of mere books. You will find more and more as the years go by, that people will gradually lay aside books, and study the nature of man in a way they have never done as yet. I tell you, then, that in this interruption of the regular school work you have not lost anything:—you have gained; you have had your minds awakened, your faculties strengthened, and your hands guided.

I do not wish to speak of this matter egotistically, but it is true that I have heard a great many persons from elsewhere mention the pleasure which they have received in meeting Tuskegee students, because when they come in contact with a student who has been here, they are impressed with the fact that he or she does not seem to be dead or sleepy. They say that when they meet a Tuskegee boy or girl they find a person who has had contact with real life. The education that you have been getting during the last few days, you will find, as the years go by, has been of a kind that will serve you in good stead all through your lives.

Just in proportion as we learn to execute something, to put our education into tangible form—as we have been doing during the last few days—in just the same proportion will we find ourselves of value as individuals and as a race. Those people who came here to visit us knew perfectly well that we could commit to memory certain lines of poetry, they knew we were able to solve certain problems in algebra and geometry, they understood that we could learn certain rules in chemistry and agriculture; but what interested them most was to see us put into visible form the results of our education. Just in proportion as an individual is able to do that, he is of value to the world. That is the object of the work which we are trying to do here. We are trying to turn out men and women who are able to do something that the world wants done, that the world needs to have done. Just in proportion as you can comply with that demand you will find that there is a place for you—there is going to be standing room. By the training we are giving you here we are preparing you for a place in the world. We are going to train you so that when you get to that place, if you fail in it, the failure will not be our fault.

It is a great satisfaction to have connected with a race men and women who are able to do something, not merely to talk about doing it, not merely to theorize about doing it, but actually to do something that makes the world better to live in, something that enhances the comforts and conveniences of life. I had a good example of this last week. I wanted something done in my office which required a practical knowledge of electricity. It was a great satisfaction when I called upon one of the teachers, to have him do the work in a careful, praiseworthy manner. It is very well to talk or lecture about electricity, but it is better to be able to do something of value with one's knowledge of electricity.

And so, as you go on, increasing your ability to do things of value, you will find that the problem which often now-a-days looks more and more difficult of solution will gradually become easier. One of the Cabinet members who were here a few days ago said, after witnessing the exhibition which you made here, that the islands which this country had taken into its possession during the recent war are soon going to require the service of every man and woman we can turn out from this institution. You will find it true, not only in this country but in other countries, that the demand will be more and more for people who can do something. Just in proportion as we can, as a race, get the reputation which I spoke to you about a few days ago, you will find there will be places for us. Regardless of colour or condition, the world is going to give the places of trust and remuneration to the men and women who can do a certain thing as well as anybody else or better. This is the whole problem. Shall we prepare ourselves to do something as well as anybody else or better? Just in proportion as we do this, you will find that nothing under the sun will keep us back.

The Importance of Being Reliable

I am going to call your attention this evening to a tendency of the people of our race which I had occasion to notice in the course of a visit recently made to certain portions of North Carolina and South Carolina.

I find that with persons who are the employers or who might be the employers of numbers of our people, there is a very general impression that as a race we lack steadiness—that we lack steadiness as labourers. Now you may say that this is not true, and you may cite any number of instances to show that we are not unreliable in that respect; whether it is true or not, the results are the same;—it works against us in the matter of securing paying employment.

Almost without exception, in talking with persons who are in a position to employ us, or who have been employing us, or who are thinking of employing us, I have found that this objection has been very largely in their minds,—that we cannot be depended upon, that we are unsteady and unreliable in matters of labour. I am speaking, of course, of that class of people of our race who depend mainly upon a day's work—working by the day, as we call it—for their living. These men with whom I talked gave several illustrations of this tendency. In the first place, I think they mentioned, without exception, this fact—that if the coloured people are employed in a factory, they work well and steadily for a few days, say until Saturday night comes, and they are paid their week's wages. Then they cannot be depended upon to put in an appearance the following Monday morning.

That special criticism was made without exception. The coloured people, these men said, would work earnestly, and give good satisfaction until they got a little money ahead, and got food enough assured to last them two or three weeks; then they would give up the job, or simply remain away from the factory until others had been put in their places. That was one of the statements that was made to me over and over again.

People also mentioned to me as an unfavourable tendency the inclination which the people of our race have to go on excursions. They said that if an excursion were going to Wilmington or Greensboro, or Charleston, and the coloured people had a little money on hand, you could not depend on their going to work instead of going on the excursion; that people would say that they must go on this or that excursion, and that nothing should stop them. A great many people lose employment and money because of this tendency to go on excursions.

Another thing that was mentioned to me was the Sunday dinners. Our people are too likely to starve all through the week, and then on Sunday invite all the neighbours to come in and eat up what they have made through the week. People say that we take our week's earnings on Saturday night, and go to the market and spend it all, and then invite all of our kindred and neighbours to come in on Sunday to have a great party. Then by Monday morning we have made ourselves so ill by overeating that we are unfit for work. This was given as one of the reasons which cause people to complain of our race for unsteadiness.

Then there was complaint of a general lack of perseverance, of an unwillingness to be steady, to put money into the bank, to begin at the bottom and gradually work toward the top. You can easily see some of the results of such a reputation as this. I have noticed some of the results in many of the places where our people have been securing paying employment. One result is a general distrust of the entire race in matters pertaining to industry. Another is that people are not going to employ persons on whom they cannot depend, to fill responsible positions. Employers are not likely to employ for responsible positions persons who are likely to go away unexpectedly on excursions.

Another result is loss of money. You will find many of our people in poverty simply because, in so large a measure, we have got this reputation of being unsteady and unreliable. Wherever our people are not getting regular, paying employment, it is largely on account of these things of which I have been speaking; and gradually the opportunities for employment are slipping into the hands of the people of other races. You can easily understand that where people are not getting steady employment—but a job this week and a job next week, and perhaps nothing the week after—it is impossible for them to put money in the bank, impossible to acquire homes and property, and to settle down as reliable, prosperous citizens.

Now, how are we going to change all these things? I do not see any hope unless we can depend upon you to change them, you young men and young women who are being educated in institutions of learning. It rests largely with you to change public sentiment among our people in all these directions, to a point where we shall feel that we must be as reliable and as responsible as it is possible for the people of any other race to be. But in order to do this it is necessary for you to learn how to control yourselves in these respects. Young men come here and want to work at this industry or that, for a while, and then get tired and want to change to something else. Some come with a strong determination to work, and stay until something happens that is not quite pleasant, and then they want to leave and go to some other school or go back home. Now we cannot make the leaders and the examples of our people that we should make, if we are going to be guilty of these same weaknesses in these institutions. Let each of you take control of himself or herself, and determine that whatever you plan to be you are going to be; you are going to keep driving away, pegging away, moving on and on each hour, each day, until you have accomplished the purpose for which you came here.

Such are the persons, the men and women, that the world is looking for. These are the men and women we want to send to North Carolina and South Carolina, to Georgia, to Mississippi, and about in our own State of Alabama, to reach hundreds and thousands of our people, and to bring about such a sentiment that these people can control themselves in the directions I have mentioned and become steady and reliable along all the avenues of industry.

I have spoken very plainly about these things, because I believe that they are matters to which as a race we ought to give more attention. No race can thrive and prosper and grow strong if it is living on the outer edges of the industrial world, is jumping here and there after a job that somebody else has given up. At the risk of repeating myself, I say that we must give attention to this matter,—we must be more trustworthy and more reliable in matters of labour. As you go home, and go into your churches, your schools and your families, preach, teach and talk from day to day the doctrine that our people must become steady and reliable, must become worthy of confidence in all their occupations.

I am sorry to say that it is too often true of young people that they overlook these matters in their conversation. We are always ready to talk about Mars and Jupiter, about the sun and moon, and about things under the earth and over the earth—in fact about everything except these little matters that have so much to do with our real living. Now if we cannot put a spirit of determination into you to go out and change public sentiment, then the future for us as a race is not very bright.

But I have faith in you to believe that you are going to set a high standard for yourselves in all these matters, and that if you can stay here two, four, five years, some of you will control yourselves in all these respects, and will bring yourselves to be examples of what we hope and expect the people whom you are going to teach are to become. If you will do this you will find that in a few years there will be a decided change for the better in the things of which I have spoken, a change in regard to these matters that will make us as a race firmer and stronger in these important directions.

The Highest Education

It may seem to some of you that I am continually talking to you about education—the right kind of education, how to get an education, and such kindred subjects—but surely no subject could be more pertinent, since the object for which you all are here is to get an education; and if you are to do this, you wish to get the best kind possible.

You will understand, then, I am sure, if I speak often about this, or refer to the subject frequently, that it is because I am very anxious that all of you go out from here with a definite and correct idea of what is meant by education, of what an education is meant to accomplish, what it may be expected to do for one.

We are very apt to get the idea that education means the memorizing of a number of dates, of being able to state when a certain battle took place, of being able to recall with accuracy this event or that event. We are likely to get the impression that education consists in being able to commit to memory a certain number of rules in grammar, a certain number of rules in arithmetic, and in being able to locate correctly on the earth's surface this mountain or that river, and to name this lake and that gulf.

Now I do not mean to disparage the value of this kind of training, because among the things that education should do for us is to give us strong, orderly and well developed minds. I do not wish to have you get the idea that I undervalue or overlook the strengthening of the mind. If there is one person more than another who is to be pitied, it is the individual who is all heart and no head. You will see numbers of persons going through the world whose hearts are full of good things— running over with the wish to do something to make somebody better, or the desire to make somebody happier—but they have made the sad mistake of being absolutely without development of mind to go with this willingness of heart. We want development of mind and we want strengthening of the mind.

I have often said to you that one of the best things that education can do for an individual is to teach that individual to get hold of what he wants, rather than to teach him how to commit to memory a number of facts in history or a number of names in geography. I wish you to feel that we can give you here orderliness of mind—I mean a trained mind—that will enable you to find dates in history or to put your finger on names in geography when you want them. I wish to give you an education that will enable you to construct rules in grammar and arithmetic for yourselves. That is the highest kind of training.

But, after all, this kind of thing is not the end of education. What, then, do we mean by education? I would say that education is meant to give us an idea of truth. Whatever we get out of text books, whatever we get out of industry, whatever we get here and there from any sources, if we do not get the idea of truth at the end, we do not get education. I do not care how much you get out of history, or geography, or algebra, or literature, I do not care how much you have got out of all your text books:—unless you have got truth, you have failed in your purpose to be educated. Unless you get the idea of truth so pure that you cannot be false in anything, your education is a failure.

Then education is meant to make us just in our dealings with our fellow men. The man or woman who has learned to be absolutely just, so far as he can interpret, has, in that degree, an education, is to that degree an educated man or woman. Education is meant to make us change for the better, to make us more thoughtful, to make us so broad that we will not seek to help one man because he belongs to this race or that race of people, and seek to hinder another man because he does not belong to this race or that race of people.

Education in the broadest and truest sense will make an individual seek to help all people, regardless of race, regardless of colour, regardless of condition. And you will find that the person who is most truly educated is the one who is going to be kindest, and is going to act in the gentlest manner toward persons who are unfortunate, toward the race or the individual that is most despised. The highly educated person is the one who is the most considerate of those individuals who are less fortunate. I hope that when you go out from here, and meet persons who are afflicted by poverty, whether of mind or body, or persons who are unfortunate in any way, that you will show your education by being just as kind and just as considerate toward those persons as it is possible for you to be. That is the way to test a person with education. You may see ignorant persons, who, perhaps, think themselves educated, going about the street, who, when they meet an individual who is unfortunate—lame, or with a defect of body, mind or speech—are inclined to laugh at and make sport of that individual. But the highly educated person, the one who is really cultivated, is gentle and sympathetic to everyone.

Education is meant to make us absolutely honest in dealing with our fellows. I don't care how much arithmetic we have, or how many cities we can locate;—it all is useless unless we have an education that makes us absolutely honest.

Education is meant to make us give satisfaction, and to get satisfaction out of giving it. It is meant to make us get happiness out of service for our fellows. And until we get to the point where we can get happiness and supreme satisfaction out of helping our fellows, we are not truly educated. Education is meant to make us generous. In this connection let me say that I very much hope that when you go out from here you will show that you have learned this lesson of being generous in all charitable objects, in the support of your churches, your Sunday schools, your hospitals, and in being generous in giving help to the poor.

I hope, for instance, that a large proportion of you—in fact all of you—will make it a practice to give something yearly to this institution. If you cannot give but twenty-five cents, fifty cents, or a dollar a year, I hope you will put it down as a thing that you will not forget, to give something to this institution every year. We want to show to our friends who have done so much for us, who have supported this school so generously, how much interest we take in the institution that has given us so nearly all that we possess. I hope that every senior, in particular, will keep this in mind. I am glad to say that we have many graduates who send us such sums, even if small, and one graduate who for the last eight or ten years has sent us ten dollars annually. I hope a number of you in the senior class that I see before me will do the same thing.

Education is meant to make us appreciate the things that are beautiful in nature. A person is never educated until he is able to go into the swamps and woods and see something that is beautiful in the trees and shrubs there, is able to see something beautiful in the grass and flowers that surround him, is, in short, able to see something beautiful, elevating and inspiring in everything that God has created. Not only should education enable us to see the beauty in these objects which God has put about us, but it is meant to influence us to bring beautiful objects about us. I hope that each one of you, after you graduate, will surround himself at home with what is beautiful, inspiring and elevating. I do not believe that any person is educated so long as he lives in a dirty, miserable shanty. I do not believe that any person is educated until he has learned to want to live in a clean room made attractive with pictures and books, and with such surroundings as are elevating.

In a word, I wish to say again, that education is meant to give us that culture, that refinement, that taste which will make us deal truthfully with our fellow men, and will make us see what is beautiful, elevating and inspiring in what God has created. I want you to bear in mind that your text books, with all their contents, are not an end, but a means to an end, a means to help us get the highest, the best, the purest and the most beautiful things out of life.

Unimproved Opportunities

S everal of the things which I shall say to you to-night may not sound very agreeable or encouraging to many of you, yet I think you will agree with me that they are facts that cannot be denied.

We must recognize the fact, in the first place, that our condition as a race is, in a large measure, different from the condition of the white race by which we are surrounded; that our capacity is very largely different from that of the people of the white race. I know we like to say the opposite. It sounds well in compositions, does well in rhetoric, and makes a splendid essay, for us to make the opposite assertion. It does very well in a newspaper article, but when we come down to hard facts we must acknowledge that our condition and capacity are not equal to those of the majority of the white people with whom we come in daily contact.

Of course that does not sound very well; but to say that we are equal to the whites is to say that slavery was no disadvantage to us. That is the logic of it. To illustrate. Suppose a person has been confined in a sick room, deprived of the use of his faculties, the use of his body and senses, and that he comes out and is placed by the side of a man who has been healthy in body and mind. Are these two persons in the same condition? Are they equal in capacity? Is the young animal of a week old, although he has all the characteristics that his mother has, as strong as she? With proper development he will be, in time, as strong as she, but it is unreasonable to say that he is as strong at present. And so, I think, this is all that we can say of ourselves—with proper development our condition and capacity will be the same as those of the people of any other race.

Now, the fact that our capacity as a people is different, and that the conditions which we must meet are different, makes it reasonable for us to believe that, when the question of education is considered, we shall find that different educational methods are desirable for us from those which would be appropriate to the needs of a people whose capacity and conditions are different from ours. What we most need, in my opinion, for the next few generations, is such an education as will help us most effectually to conquer the forces of nature;—I mean in the general sense of supplying food, clothing, homes, and a substantial provision for the future.

Do not think that I mean by this that I do not believe in every individual getting all the education, he or she can get,—for I do. But since for some years to come, at least, it must of necessity be impossible for all of our young people to get all the education possible, or even all they may want to get, I believe they should apply their energies to getting such a training as will be best fitted to supply their immediate needs.

In Scotland, for instance, where higher education has been within reach of the people for many years, and where the people have reached a high degree of civilization, it is not out of place for the young people to give their time and attention to the study of metaphysics and of law and the other professions. Of course I do not mean to say that we shall not have lawyers and metaphysicians and other professional men after a while, but I do mean to say that I think the efforts of a large majority of us should be devoted to securing the material necessities of life.

When you speak to the average person about labor—industrial work, especially—he seems to get the idea at once that you are opposed to his head being educated—that you simply wish to put him to work. Anybody that knows anything about industrial education knows that it teaches a person just the opposite—how not to work. It teaches him to make water work for him,—air, steam, all the forces of nature. That is what is meant by industrial education.

Let us make an illustration. Yesterday I was over in the creamery and became greatly interested in the process of separating the cream. The only energy spent was that required to turn a crank. The apparatus had been so constructed as to utilize natural forces. Now compare the old process of butter-making with the new. Before, you had to go through a long process of drudgery before the cream could be separated from the milk, and then another long process before the cream could be turned into butter, and then, even after churning three or four hours at a time, you got only a small portion of butter. Now what we mean by giving you an industrial education is to teach you so to put brains into your work that if your work is butter-making, you can make butter simply by standing at a machine and turning a crank.

If you are studying chemistry, be sure you get all you can out of the course here, and then go to a higher school somewhere else. Become as proficient in the science as you can. When you have done this, do not sit down and wait for the world to honour you because you know a great deal about chemistry—you will be disappointed if you do—but if you wish to make the best use of your knowledge of chemistry, come back here to the South and use it in making this poor soil rich, and in making good butter where the farmers have made poor butter before. Used in this way you will find that your knowledge of chemistry will cause others to honour you.

During the last thirty years we, as a race, have let some golden opportunities slip from us, and partly, I fear, because we have not had enough plain talk in the direction I am following with you to-night. If you ever have an opportunity to go into any of the large cities of the North you will be able to see for yourselves what I mean. I remember that the first time I went North—and it was not so very many years ago—it was not an uncommon thing to see the barber shops in the hands of coloured men. I know coloured men who in that way could have become comfortably rich. You cannot find to-day in the city of New York or Boston a first-class barber shop in the hands of coloured men. That opportunity is gone, and something is wrong that it is so. Coming nearer home; go to Montgomery, Memphis, New Orleans, and you will find that the barber shops are gradually slipping away from the hands of the coloured men, and they are going back into dark streets and opening little holes. These opportunities have slipped from us largely because we have not learned to dignify labour. The coloured man puts a dirty little chair and a pair of razors into a dirtier looking hole, while the white man opens his shop on one of the principal streets, or in connection with some fashionable hotel, fits it up luxuriously with carpets, handsome mirrors and other attractive furniture, and calls the place a "tonsorial parlour." The proprietor sits at his desk and takes the cash. He has transformed what we call drudgery into a paying business.

Still another instance. You can remember that only a few years ago one of the best paying positions that a large number of coloured men filled was that of doing whitewashing. A few years ago it would not have been hard to see coloured men in Boston, Philadelphia or Washington carrying a whitewash tub and a long pole into somebody's house to do a job of whitewashing. You go into the North to-day, and you will find very few coloured men at that work. White men learned that they could dignify that branch of labour, and they began to study it in schools. They gained a knowledge of chemistry which would enable them to understand the mixing of the necessary ingredients; they learned decorating and frescoing; and now they call themselves "house decorators." Now that job is gone, perhaps to come no more; for now that these men have elevated this work, and introduced more intelligent skill into it, do you suppose any one is going to allow some old man with a pole and a bucket to come into the house?

Then there is the field occupied by the cooks. You know that all over the South we have held—and still hold to a large extent—the matter of cooking in our hands. Wherever there was any cooking to be done, a coloured man or a coloured woman did it. But while we still have something of a monopoly of this work, it is a fact that even this is slipping away from us. People do not wish always to eat fried meat, and bread that is made almost wholly of water and salt. They get tired of such food, and they desire a person to cook for them who will put brains into the work. To met this demand white people have transformed what was once the menial occupation of cooking into a profession; they have gone to school and studied how to elevate this work, and if we can judge by the almost total absence of coloured cooks in the North, we are led to believe that they have learned how. Even here in the South coloured cooks are gradually disappearing, and unless they exert themselves they will go entirely. They have disappeared in the North because they have not kept pace with the demand for the most improved methods of cooking, and because they have not realized that the world is moving forward rapidly in the march of civilization. A few days ago, when in Chicago, I noticed in one of the fashionable restaurants a fine-looking man, well dressed, who seemed to be the proprietor. I asked who he was, and was told that he was the "chef," as he is called—the head cook. Of course I was surprised to see a man dressed so stylishly and presenting such an air of culture, filling the place of chief cook in a restaurant, but I remembered then, more forcibly than ever, that cooking had been transformed into a profession—into dignified labour.

Still another opportunity is going, and we laugh when we mention it, although it is really no laughing matter. When we think of what we might have done to elevate it in the same way that white persons have elevated it, we realize that it was an opportunity after all. I refer to the opportunity which was in boot-blacking. Of course, here in the South, we have that yet, to a large extent, because the competition here is not quite so sharp as in the North. In too many Southern towns and cities, if you wish your shoes blacked, you wait until you meet a boy with a box slung over his shoulder. When he begins to polish your shoes you will very likely see that he uses a much-worn shoe brush, or, worse still, a scrubbing brush, and unless you watch him closely there is a chance that he will polish your shoes with stove polish. But if you go into a Northern city you will find that such a boy as this does not stand a chance of making a living. White boys and even men have opened shops which they have fitted up with carpets, pictures, mirrors, and comfortable chairs, and sometimes their brushes are even run by electricity. They have the latest newspapers always within reach for their patrons to read while their work is being done, and they grow rich. The man who owns and runs such a place as that is not called a "boot-black"; he is called the proprietor of such and such a "Shoe-blacking Emporium." And that chance is gone to come no more. Now there are many coloured men who understand about electricity, but where is the coloured man who would apply his knowledge of that science to running brushes in a boot-black stand?

In the South it was a common thing when anybody was taken ill to notify the old mammy nurse. We had a monopoly of the nursing business for many years, and up to a short time ago it was the common opinion that nobody could nurse but one of those old black mammies. But this idea is being dissipated. In the North, when a person gets ill, he does not think of sending for any one but a professional nurse, one who has received a diploma from some nurse-training school, or a certificate of proficiency from some reputable institution.

I hope you have understood me in what I have been trying to say of these little things. They all tend to show that if we are to keep pace with the progress of civilization, we must pay attention to the small things as well as the larger and more important things in life. They go to prove that we must put brains into what we do. If education means anything at all, it means putting brains into the common affairs of life and making something of them. That is just what we are seeking to tell to the world through the work of this institution.

There are many opportunities all about us where we can use our education. You very rarely see a man idle who knows all about house-building, who knows how to draw plans, to test the strength of materials that enter into the making of a first-class house. Did you ever see such a man out of a job? Did you ever see such a man as that writing letters to this place and that place applying for work? People are wanted all over the world who can do work well. Men and women are wanted who understand the preparation and supplying of food—I don't mean in the small menial sense—but people who know all about it. Even in this there is a great opportunity. A few days ago I met a woman who had spent years in this country and in Europe studying the subject of food economics in all its details. I learn that this person is in constant demand by institutions of learning and other establishments where the preparation and the serving of food are important features. She spends a few months at each institution. She is wanted everywhere, because she has applied her education to one of the most important necessities of life.

And so you will find it all through life—those persons who are going to be constantly sought after, constantly in demand, are those who make the best use of their opportunities, who work unceasingly to become proficient in whatever they attempt to do. Always be sure that you have something out of which you can make a living, and then you will not only be independent, but you will be in a much better position to help your fellow-men.

I have spoken about these matters at this length because I believe them to be the foundation of our future success. We often hear a man spoken of as having moral character. A man cannot have moral character unless he has something to wear, and something to eat three hundred and sixty-five days in a year. He cannot have any religion either. You will find at the bottom of much crime the fact that the criminals have not had the common necessities of life supplied them. Men must have some of the comforts and conveniences—certainly the necessities of life—supplied them before they can be morally or religiously what they ought to be.

Keeping Your Word

I do not want to speak to you continually upon subjects that tend to show up the weaker traits of character which our race has, but there are some characteristic points in our life so important that it seems to me well that we emphasize those which are specially weak just now.

A few weeks ago I mentioned two or three examples which had come under my own personal observation, of the unreliability of the race, and to those I now add one or two more.

On three distinct occasions, while travelling, I have found it necessary to make engagements with hackmen to call at a certain hour in the morning to take me to an early train, and on no one of these occasions has the hackman kept his word. In the first case the man disappointed me entirely, so that I had to walk to the station, a distance of a mile or more. In the second instance the hackman was to come at six o'clock, and did not come until half-past six. By that time I had started to walk, and had gone two or three squares, meeting him on the way to the place where I had stopped. In the third case the man was at least an hour late when we met him, after we had walked over half the distance to the station.

I have spoken at another time of the fact that men who employ coloured workmen have complained to me that after these men had drawn a week's pay, they could not be depended upon to return to work the next Monday morning. In the city of Savannah, Georgia, there are a great many coloured men employed as stevedores—men who load and unload ships. If you have read the newspapers carefully you will have noticed that recently the persons who employ these men have made a new rule, by which they refuse to pay the stevedores all of their wages at the end of the week, but retain two days' pay out of each week, from every individual who works for them, to be paid to them at the end of the next week. Of course the men do not lose anything in the end by this method; it simply means that so long as they work for one employer there are at least two days' pay due them. Of course the labourers whose wages were thus kept back have made a great noise about it, but when their employers were asked for an explanation, they said: "We find by experience that if we pay you all that we owe you on Saturday night, we cannot depend upon your returning on Monday morning to continue your work. You are apt to get drunk, or to debauch yourselves on Sunday so that you are unfitted for your work the next day." This is the decision these men have arrived at after having employed these men for a number of years.

Now think of the things I have spoken to you about. You may say with regard to the last, that to a great extent this action on the part of the Savannah employers was due to prejudice, to a desire to use the money withheld for their own selfish purposes, and because they had the power to do so, but you can very easily understand that if a person goes on being disappointed month after month in his business, he will soon conclude that it is best for him to try a hackman of some other colour and disposition, and that if these Savannah employers find year after year that they cannot depend on coloured men to give them thorough, regular, systematic labour, they are going to look out for persons of another race who will do their work properly.

It is not necessary for me to continue in this strain, and to call attention to other incidents of this kind, to show, as I have told you before, that one of the weak points which we as a race must fight against, is that of not being reliable. Of course I understand that it is not always possible for a person to keep an engagement, but if he cannot, it is very rarely the case that he cannot send word to the person with whom he has made the engagement of his inability to keep his part of it. In the case of the hackmen who disappointed me, if they had sent word two or three hours ahead of the time, that they could not come, or if they had sent another hackman to fill the engagement for them, I should have thought nothing about it. In the case of those Savannah labourers, when they found they could not go back to their work promptly, if they had sent word to that effect, their absence, perhaps, could have been excused. But it is this habit of disappointing people in business matters without apparent care or concern that has given the race the damaging reputation which it has for unreliability.

I speak of these things repeatedly and so plainly because I am constantly meeting persons who are employers or who would be employers of our people, and they tell me every time when I speak to them about work, that their only objection to employing coloured labour is this very matter I have been speaking of, its unreliability. Many of them say that they want to employ coloured people, would be glad to give them places of responsibility, but that they cannot find men who will stick to their work.

You may say that it is impossible for us to grow and develop, to get positions of trust and responsibility that will pay good wages, simply because we are coloured. I will give you an example on this very point. A few days ago I was in New Orleans, visiting a large sugar refinery. The firm which operates this refinery employs from two hundred to three hundred men. I found the young man who has charge of all the bookkeeping of the firm, through whose hands all the business and cash of the firm pass—I found this man to be coloured, and that all the other persons filling responsible positions under him were white.

I remember some two or three years ago having met one of the partners of this firm in the White Mountains, and he told me at that time of this young man. He told me that a great many persons came to him and said: "You ought not to have this coloured man filling this position when there are so many white persons who want the place." He told me that he said to these persons: "This young man does my work better than any one else I have yet found, and so long as he does this, so long shall I employ him." This gentleman has since died, but the business is in the hands of his widow, who has so much confidence in the ability of this young coloured man to manage the affairs of a great business—Mr. Lewis is his name; perhaps some of you know him—that he is retained, practically at the head of this great establishment. This single instance shows that notwithstanding his colour a man can rise for what is in him; that he can advance when he shows that he can be depended upon.

Remember that whether you are hackmen, or business men, it pays whenever you cannot fill an engagement to explain beforehand why you cannot, and that unless you make a practice of doing this, it will be impossible for you to get ahead or to attain to places of trust and responsibility, no matter how much education you may have.

As I have so often said before, if we cannot send out from Tuskegee and similar schools young men and women who can be depended upon, our reputation as a race, for the years that are to come, is not going to be very bright. On the other hand, if we can succeed in sending out young men and women with a high sense of responsibility, who can at all times be relied upon to be prompt in business matters, we shall have gone a long way in redeeming the character of the race and in lifting it up. In this important matter all of you can help. Do not wait until you go out from Tuskegee, but begin to-morrow morning, every boy and girl, to be reliable and to keep at it until reliability becomes a part of you.

Some Lessons of the Hour

This evening I am going to remind you of a few things which you should get out of the school year, but it will be of very little use for me to do this unless you make up your minds to do two things.

In the first place you must resolve that you are going to remember the things I am going to say, and in the second place you must put my suggestions into practice. If you will make up your minds, then, that you are going to hold on to these suggestions, so far as your memory is concerned, and then so far as possible put them into practice, we shall be able to discuss something that will be of profit to you during the year.

I want you to get it firmly fixed in your minds that books, industries, or tools of any character, no matter how thoroughly you master them, do not within themselves constitute education. Committing to memory pages of written matter, or becoming deft in the handling of tools, is not the supreme thing at which education aims. Books, tools, and industries are but the means to fit you for something that is higher and better. All these are not ends within themselves; they are simply means. The end of all education, whether of head or hand or heart, is to make an individual good, to make him useful, to make him powerful; is to give him goodness, usefulness and power in order that he may exert a helpful influence upon his fellows.

One of the things I want you to get out of this year is the ability to put a proper value upon time. If there is any one lesson that we all of us need to have impressed upon us more thoroughly and more constantly than any other, it is that each minute of our lives is of supreme value, and that we are committing a sin when we allow a single minute to go to waste. Remember that every five minutes of time you are spending at this institution is worth so much money to you. How many people there are who, after they have arrived at the ages of sixty, seventy, or eighty years, look back with regret and say, "I wish I could live the years over again." But they cannot. All they can do is to regret that they have wasted precious minutes, precious hours.

Now your lives are yet before you, not, as in the case of these people, behind you. Your lives are yet to be lived, and they will be made successful lives just in proportion as you learn to place a value upon the minutes. Spend every minute here in hard, earnest study, or in helpful recreation. Be sure that none of your time is thrown away.

BOOKER T. WASHINGTON

Among other things, you should get out of the year the habit of reading. Any individual who has learned to love good books, to love the best newspapers, the best magazines, and has learned to spend some portion of the day in communication with them, is a happy individual. You should get yourselves to the point where you will not be happy unless you do spend a part of each day in this way.

You should get out of the year the habit of being kind and polite to every individual. As a general thing it is not difficult for a person to be polite in words and courteous in actions to individuals who are classed in the same social scale, or who, perhaps, are above him in wealth and influence. The test of a true lady or gentleman comes when that individual is brought in contact with some one who is considered beneath her or him, some one who is ignorant or poor. Show me a man who is himself wealthy, and who is gentle and polite to the ignorant about him, and to the poor people about him, and I will show you every time a true gentleman. When Prince Henry of Prussia was in this country, I remember reading this description of one of the prominent public men who received him: "He is such a true gentleman that he can meet a prince without himself being embarrassed, and can meet a poor man without embarrassing the poor man."

Learn to speak kindly to every individual, white or black. No man loses anything by being gentlemanly, by learning to be polite, by treating the most unfortunate individual with the highest deference.

We want you to learn to control your temper. Some one has said that the difference between an animal and a man is that the beast has no method of learning to control his temper. With the individual, the human being, there is education and training. He learns to master himself, to have an even temper; learns to master his temper completely. Now if any of you have a temper that often gets to be your master, make up your mind that it is a part of your duty here to learn to control it. Step upon it, as it were, and say: "I will be master of my temper, instead of letting it be my master."

You want to have that kind of courage that is going to make you able to speak the truth at all times, no matter what it may seem to cost you. This may, for the time being, seem to make you unpopular; it may inconvenience you, it may deprive you of something that you count dear; but the individual who cultivates that kind of courage, who, at the cost of everything, always speaks the truth, is the individual who in the end will be successful, is the one who in the end will come out the conqueror. You cannot afford to learn to speak anything but the absolute truth. One of the most beautiful things that I have seen printed about President Roosevelt was where someone wrote of him that one of the President's greatest faults was that he did not know when to lie—when to deceive people—but that he always spoke the absolute, frank truth. As a result of his honesty, his truth speaking, he is at the head of the nation.

We also want you to learn to be absolutely honest in all your dealings with other people's property. We may just as well speak plainly and emphatically. One of our worst sins, one of our weaknesses, is that of not being able to handle other people's property and be honest with it. You should learn to be absolutely honest with the property of your room-mates, school-mates and teachers. Make up your minds that nothing is going to tempt you from the path of absolute honesty. There is no man or woman who begins with meddling with other people's property and affairs, who begins to learn to take that which does not belong to him or her, who is not beginning in a downward path ending in misery, sorrow and disappointment. Make up your minds that you are going to be absolutely honest and truthful in all cases. There is no way to get happiness out of life, there is no way to get satisfaction out of your school career, except by following the lessons that I have here tried to emphasize.

When we speak of honesty, the first thought may be that the word applies only to the taking of property that does not belong to us, but this is not so. It is possible for a person to be dishonest by taking time or energy that belongs to someone else, just as much as tangible property. In going into a class-room, office, store or shop, one man may ask himself the question: "How little can I do to-day and still get through the day?" Another man will have constantly before him the question: "How much can I put into this hour or this day?" Now we expect every student who goes out from Tuskegee to be, not the man who tries to see how little he can do, or the average man who proposes to do merely his duty, but the man above the average, who will do more than his duty. And you will disappoint us unless you are above the average man, unless you go out from here with the determination that you are going to perform more than your duty.

I like to see young men or young women who, if employed in any capacity, no matter how small or unimportant that capacity may be, if the hour is eight o'clock at which they must come to work, I like to see them at work ten or fifteen minutes before that hour. I like to see a man or woman who, if the closing hour is five o'clock or six o'clock, goes to the person in charge and says: "Shall I not stay longer? Is there not something else I ought to do before I go?" Put your whole souls into whatever you attempt to do. That is honesty.

Another thing you should learn this year is to get into touch with the best people there are in the world. You should learn to associate with the best students in the institution. Take them as models, and say that you are going to improve from month to month, and from year to year, until you are as good as they are, or better. You cannot reach these things all at once, but I hope that each one of you will make up his mind or her mind that from to-night, throughout the year and throughout life, there is going to be a hard striving on your part toward reaching the best results. If you do this, when you get ready to leave this institution, you will find that it has been worth your while to have spent your time here.

The Gospel of Service

The subject on which I am going to speak to you for a few minutes to-night, "The Gospel of Service," may not, when you first hear it, strike a very responsive chord in your hearts and minds, but I assure you I have nothing but the very highest and best interest of the race at heart when I select this subject to talk about.

The word "service" has too often been misunderstood, and on this account it has in too many cases carried with it a meaning which indicates degradation. Every individual serves another in some capacity, or should do so. Christ said that he who would become the greatest of all must become the servant of all; that is, He meant that in proportion as one renders service he becomes great. The President of the United States is a servant of the people, because he serves them; the Governor of Alabama is a servant, because he renders service to the people of the State; the greatest merchant in Montgomery is a servant, because he renders service to his customers; the school teacher is a servant, because it is his duty to serve the best interests of his pupils; the cook is a servant, because it is her duty to serve those for whom she works; the housemaid is a servant, because it is her duty to care for the property intrusted to her in the best manner in which she is able.

In one way or another, every individual who amounts to anything is a servant. The man or the woman who is not a servant is one who accomplishes nothing. It is very often true that a race, like an individual, does not appreciate the opportunities that are spread out before it until those opportunities have disappeared. Before us, as a race in the South to-day, there is a vast field for service and usefulness which is still in our hands, but which I fear will not be ours to the same extent very much longer unless we change our ideas of service, and put new life, put new dignity and intelligence into it.

Perhaps I am right in thinking that in no department of life has there been such great progress and such changes for the better during the last ten years as in the department of domestic service, or housekeeping. The cook who does not make herself intelligent, who does not learn to do things in the latest, and in the neatest and cleanest manner, will soon find herself without employment, or will at least find herself a "drug on the market," instead of being sought after and paid higher wages. The woman who does not keep up with all the latest methods of decorating and setting her table, and of putting the food on it properly, will find her occupation gone within a few years. The same is true of general housekeeping, of laundering and of nursing.

All the occupations of which I have been talking are at present in our hands in the South; but I repeat that very great progress is being made in all of them in every part of the world, and we shall find that we shall lose them unless our women go forward and get rid of the old idea that such occupations are fit only for ignorant people to follow. At the present time scores of books and magazines are appearing bearing upon every branch of domestic service. People are learning to do things in an intelligent and scientific manner. Not long ago I sat for an hour and listened to a lecture delivered upon the subject of dusting, and it was one of the most valuable hours I ever spent. The person who gave this lecture upon dusting was a highly educated and a cultivated woman, and her audience was composed of wealthy and cultivated people. We must bring ourselves to the point where we can feel that one who cooks, and does it well, should be just as much honoured as the person who teaches school.

What I have said in regard to the employments of our women is equally true of the occupations followed by our men. It is true that at the present we are largely cultivating the soil of the South, but if other people learn to do this work more intelligently, learn more about labour-saving machinery, and become more conscientious about their work than we, we shall find our occupation departing. It used to be the case in many parts of the North that the Negro was the coachman; but in a very large degree, in cities like New York and Philadelphia, the Negro has lost this occupation, and lost it, in my opinion, not because he was a Negro, but because in many cases he did not see that the occupation of coachman was constantly being improved. It has been improved and lifted up until now it has almost become a profession. The Negro who expects to remain a coachman should learn the proper dress for a coachman, and learn how to care for horses and vehicles in the most approved manner.

What is true of the coachman is true of the butler. In too many cases, I fear, we use these occupations merely as stepping stones, holding on to them until we can find something else to do, in a careless and slipshod manner. We want to change all this, and put our whole souls into these occupations, and in a large degree make them our life-work. In proportion as we do this, we shall lay a foundation upon which our children and grandchildren are to rise to higher things. The foundation of every race must be laid in the common every-day occupations that are right about our doors. It should not be our thought to see how little we can put into our work, but how much; not how quickly we can get rid of our tasks, but how well we can do them.

I often wish that I had the means to put into every city a large training-school for giving instruction in all lines of domestic service. Few things would add more to the fundamental usefulness of the race than such a school. Perhaps it may be suggested that my argument has reference only to our serving white people. It has reference to doing whatever we do in the best manner, no matter whom we serve. The individual who serves a black man poorly will serve a white man poorly. Let me illustrate what I mean. In a Southern city, a few days ago, I found a large hotel conducted by coloured people. It is one of the very cleanest and best and most attractive hotels for coloured people that I have found in any part of the country. In talking with the proprietors I asked them what was the greatest obstacle they had had to overcome, and they told me it was in finding coloured women to work in the house who would do their work systematically and well, women who would, in a word, keep the rooms in every part of the hotel thoroughly swept and cleaned. This hotel had been opened three months, and I found that during that time the proprietors had employed fifteen different chambermaids, and they had got rid of a large proportion of these simply because they were determined not to have people in their employment who did not do their work well.

One weakness pertaining to the whole matter of domestic employment in the South, at present, is this: it is too easy for our people to find work. If there was a rule followed in every family that employs persons, that no man or woman should be hired unless he or she brought a letter of recommendation from the last employer, we should find that the whole matter of domestic service would be lifted up a hundred per cent. So long as an individual can do poor work for one family, and perhaps be dishonest at the same time, and be sure that he or she will be employed by some other family, without regard to the kind of service rendered the last employer, so long will domestic service be poor and unsatisfactory.

Many white people seldom come in contact with the Negro in any other capacity than that of domestic service. If they get a poor idea of our character and service in that respect, they will infer that the entire life of the Negro is unsatisfactory from every point of view. We want to be sure that wherever our life touches that of the white man, we conduct ourselves so that he will get the best impression possible of us.

In spite of all the fault I have found, I would say this before I stop. I recognize that the people of no race, under similar circumstances, have made greater progress in thirty-five years than is true of the people of the Negro race. If I have spoken to you thus plainly and frankly, it is that our progress in the future may be still greater than it has been in the past.

Your Part in the Negro Conference

For eight or nine years, now, it has been our custom to hold here what is known as the Tuskegee Negro Conference. A number of years ago it occurred to some of us that instead of confining the work of this institution to the immediate body of students gathered within its walls, we perhaps could extend and broaden its scope so as to reach out to, and try to help, the parents of the students and the older people in the country districts, and, to some extent, if possible, in the cities also.

With this end in view, we, some years ago, invited a number of men and women to come and spend the day with us, and, while here, to tell us in a very plain and straightforward manner something about their material, moral and religious condition. Then the afternoon of that same day was spent in hearing from these same men and women suggestions as to how they thought this institution and other institutions might help them, and also how they thought they might help themselves.

Out of these simple and small meetings has grown what we now call "The Tuskegee Negro Conference," which, in the last few years, has grown until it numbers from nine hundred to twelve hundred persons. We not only have that large number of persons, most of whom come from farms and are engaged in farm work, but we now also have "The Workers' Conference," which meets on the day following the Negro Conference. This Workers' Conference brings together representatives from all the larger institutions for the education of the Negro in the South.

Now these meetings for this year begin next Wednesday morning, and the practical question that I wish to discuss with you to-night is,— What can we do to make that Conference a success? What can you do for the Conference, and what can the Conference do for you?

I wish you to grasp the idea that is growing through the country— that very few institutions now confine themselves and their work to mere teaching in the class-room, in the old-fashioned manner. Very few now confine themselves and their work to the comparatively small number of students that they can reach in that way, as they did a few years ago. In many cases they have their college extension work. In one way or another they are reaching out and getting hold of the young people—and getting a hold on the older people as well. And just so, to a very large degree, through this Conference, Tuskegee is doing something of the same kind of thing.

BOOKER T. WASHINGTON

During these few days we shall have hundreds of the farmers, with their wives and daughters, gathered here. We want each and every one of you here in the institution to make up your mind that you can do something to help these people. We want each one of you here to-night to feel that he or she has a special responsibility during the time these people are gathered together at Tuskegee. We sometimes speak of it as their one day of schooling in the whole year,—that is, the one day out of the whole three hundred and sixty-five days in the year when, perhaps, they will give the greatest amount of attention to matters pertaining to themselves. In inviting them here, not only the teachers and officers of this institution have a responsibility, but each and every student here also has a responsibility. I want you to feel that, and see to what extent you can take hold of these people while they are here, to inspire and encourage them, so as to have them go away from here feeling that it is worth their while to come to the Institute for this meeting, even if—as is true of some of them—they have come a long distance.

Some of these people who will come here are ignorant, so far as books are concerned, but I want you to know that not every person who cannot read and write is ignorant. Some of the persons whom I have met and from whom I have learned much, are persons who cannot write a word. Very many of the people who will come here may not be able to read or write, but we can learn something from them notwithstanding, while they are here, and they can learn something from us.

I want you to take delight in getting hold of these people and taking them through our shops, guiding them through our various agricultural and mechanical departments. Be sure that you exert every effort possible to make them comfortable and happy while they are here. Heretofore the students have been so generous, at the time of this meeting, that many of them, if necessary, have given up their rooms that these people might have a comfortable night's rest. I do not know where you have slept, but I do not think that in the history of the school a student was ever asked to give up his room to any of these people that he did not gladly and freely do so. I believe that you are going to do the same thing this year.

I want you, also, to remember that you not only can help the Conference to be a success by being polite and kindly to the farmers who come from this and other Southern States, but also by being polite and attentive to the representatives from the large institutions that will be here. We will have present representatives from every large institution engaged in the education of our people. It means much for the principals and instructors in these large colleges and industrial schools to leave their work and come as far as many of them do, to spend these days here. We have a responsibility on their account; we desire them to feel that it has been worth their while to leave their work and spend their time and money to come here for these meetings. We wish them to get something out of our industries here; we wish them to get something out of the training here, in every department, something which they can take back to their own institution to make their work there stronger and better.

Now as to yourselves. You can get something out of this Conference for yourselves, by getting hold of everything possible, so that when you go out from Tuskegee you will have just that much more helpful information to put into practice. I want to see you go out through the South and establish local conferences. Call them together, and teach the same kind of lessons that we teach at these gatherings at Tuskegee. You can get the most out of this Conference by putting into practice this effort to make other people happy. To get the greatest happiness out of life is to make somebody else happy. To get the greatest good out of life is to do something for somebody else. I want you to find the persons who are most ignorant and most poverty stricken; I want you to find the persons who are most forlorn and most discouraged, and do something for them to make their hours happy. In doing that, you will do the most for yourselves.

I want each boy and each girl who belongs to this institution to be deep down in his or her heart a gentleman or a lady. A gentleman means simply this: a generous person; one who has learned to be kind; one who has learned to think not of himself first, but of the happiness and welfare of others. Let us put this spirit into our Conference day the coming week, and the day and week will be the greatest and most successful that we have ever had. Let our resolution be that the persons who come here, whether they represent a university, a college, an industrial school, a farm, or a shop—let our resolve be that when these people leave here they shall take away with them from Tuskegee something that will make their lives happier, brighter, stronger and more useful.

What is to be Our Future?

Last Thursday afternoon I received a telegram from a gentleman stopping for a time in a city in Georgia, asking me to come there at once on important business; and being rather curious to know what he wanted of me, I went. I found that this man was in the act of making his will, and that he had in mind the putting aside of a considerable sum in his will—some $20,000, in fact—for this institution.

The special point upon which this gentleman wished to consult me was the future of the Institution. He said that he had worked very hard for his money, that it had come as a result of much sacrifice and hard effort, and that there were friends of his who were beseeching him to use his money in other directions, because they thought it would be more likely to do permanent good elsewhere. And so he wished to know what the future of this Institution is likely to be, because he did not care to risk his money upon an uncertain venture, one that was likely to prosper for a few years, and then fail. He said that he would not like to give his money to an institution where it would not go on through the years, accomplishing a certain amount of good. Accordingly the question he repeated to me over and over again was: "What is to be the future of Tuskegee?" He wished to know whether, if we were given the money, it would go on from year to year, blessing one generation after another.

My point in speaking to you to-night is to emphasize what I think our good friend Professor Brown has already brought to our attention in one or two of his talks to us this week, the importance of making this institution what it ought to be, what its reputation gives it, and what its name implies.

More and more I realize—and I remember that the gentleman of whom I have spoken repeated this to me with great emphasis—that so far as the outside world is concerned, Tuskegee is sure; you need not have the least doubt that the institution will be supported. If we keep things right at the institution, if it is worthy of support, the moneyed people of the country will support it and stand by it. More and more each year this impression grows upon me, and more and more each year there are convincing evidences of the fact that the permanence and growth of this institution do not rest upon whether the people of the South or the people of the North are going to support it with their means. I have the most implicit confidence that the institution is going to be supported. But the question that comes to us with the greatest force is: "Are we going to be worthy of that support? Shall we be worthy of the confidence of the public?" That is the question that is most serious; that is the question that presses most heavily upon my heart, and upon the hearts of the other teachers here.

Now these questions can be answered satisfactorily only by evidence that each student, each individual connected with the school in any way, no matter in how low or high a capacity, is putting his or her whole conscience into the work here. When I say work, I mean study of books, work of the hand, effort of the body, willingness of the heart. No matter what the thing is, put your conscience into it; do your best. Let it be possible for you to say: "I have put my whole soul into my study, into my work, into whatever I have attempted. Whatever I have done I have honestly endeavored to do to the best of my ability."

The questions which this gentleman asked me, and similar kinds of questions, are being asked over and over again by people all over the country. The question can be answered only by our putting our consciences into our work, and by our being entirely unselfish in it. Let every person get into the habit of planning every day for the comfort and welfare of others, let each one try to live as unselfishly as possible, remembering that the Bible says: "He that would save his life, must lose it." And you never saw a person save his life in this higher sense, in the Christ-like sense, unless that person was willing, day by day, to lose himself in the interest of his fellow-men. Such persons save their own lives, and in saving them save thousands of other lives.

Such questions as these can be satisfactorily answered not merely by our putting our consciences into every effort, no matter what the effort may be, but by improving, day by day, upon what has been done the day before. In large institutions and establishments it is comparatively easy to find persons who will sweep a room day by day, or plough a field during certain seasons of the year, and do other work at certain other seasons of the year, but the difficulty comes in finding persons who make improvements in the manner of sweeping rooms, of ploughing fields and planting corn. The question for us is: "Are we going to put so much brains into our efforts every year, that we are going to go on steadily and constantly improving from year to year?" Are you going to get into the habit of so thinking about your work here that the habit will become, as it were, a part of yourself, so that when you go out into the world you will not be satisfied to take a position and go on in the same humdrum manner, but will not be satisfied until your work has been improved in every possible detail, and made easier, more systematic, and more convenient?

We must put brains into our work. There must be improvement in every department of this institution every year. It is absolutely impossible for an institution to stand still; it must go forward or backward, grow better or worse each year. An institution grows stronger and more useful each year, or weaker and less useful.

This institution can grow only by each person putting his thought into his work, by planning how he can improve the work of his particular department, by constantly striving to make his work more useful to the institution, by keeping the place where he works cleaner, and making his work more business-like and more systematic. That is the only way in which the questions which people all over the country are asking about this institution can be satisfactorily answered.

You will find that people will look to us more and more for tangible results. Not only here, but all over the country, our race is going to be called on to answer the question: "What can the race really accomplish?" It is perfectly well understood by our friends as well as by our enemies, that we can write good newspaper articles and make good addresses, that we can sing well and talk well, and all that kind of thing. All that is perfectly well understood and conceded. But the question that will be more and more forced upon us for an answer is: "Can we work out our thoughts, can we put them into tangible shape, so that the world may see from day to day actual evidences of our intellectuality?"

Last winter I was in the town of Clinton, Iowa. I think I had never heard of the place before, and when I got there I was surprised to find it a place of more than 16,000 inhabitants. The gentleman who was to entertain me wanted to take me to a coloured restaurant. I expected to go into a restaurant of the kind operated by our people generally, and I was very much surprised when he took me into a large, two-story building. I found the floors carpeted, and everything about the place as pleasant and attractive as it was possible to make it. In fact the restaurant compared very favourably with many in the largest cities in the country. I found the waiters clean, the service good, and everything conducted in the most systematic manner. And there was not the least thing, except the colour of the proprietor's skin, to show that the place was operated by coloured people.

Afterward my friend took me into another establishment of the same size, operated in the same creditable manner by another coloured man. In both I found that these gentlemen not only carried on a regular restaurant business, but manufactured their own candies and ice cream, and did a sort of wholesale catering business. I asked the white people there what they thought of the coloured people, and I did not find a single white person who did not have the most implicit confidence in the coloured people. The trouble was that there were not many coloured people there. That accounts possibly for the good opinion which the white people have of them. But you see what just two black men can do. These people had never seen many black people, but fortunately for us they had with them two of the best specimens of our race that I have ever seen anywhere in this country. As a result you do not find any one cursing the black man in that town. Everybody had the utmost confidence in black people, and respected them.

Just in proportion as we can establish object lessons of this kind all over the country, you will find that the problem that now is so perplexing will disappear. Until we do this, we shall not be able to talk away, or to argue away, this prejudice. We cannot talk our way into our rights; we must work our way, think our way, into them. And you will find that just in proportion as we do this, we are going to get all we deserve.

Some Great Little Things

I am going to speak to you for a few minutes to-night upon what I shall term "Some Great Little Things." I speak of them as great, because of their supreme importance, and I speak of them as little, because they come in a class of things which are usually looked upon by many people as small and unimportant. But in an institution like this I think they often hold first place—certainly they come under the head of important things that we can learn.

You will remember that in the sermon the Chaplain preached this morning, he mentioned the three-fold division of our nature; the physical part, the mental part, and the spiritual part. What I shall refer to to-night has largely to do with the material, the physical part of our natures. There are certain little things that each one of you can learn now, in connection with the care of your bodies, which, if left unlearned now, will perhaps go without being learned all your lives. You are now, as it were, at the parting of the ways—you are going to make these habits a part of yourselves, or you are going to let them escape you forever, and be weak in a measure all your lives for not having made them a part of yourselves.

I am going to speak very plainly, because I feel that such talk means nothing unless it is in language which every one can appreciate and understand. Now, among the first things that a person going to a boarding school should learn, if he has not already learned it at home—and I am constantly being surprised at the number who seem to have thus left it unlearned—is the habit of regular and systematic bathing. No person who has left this habit unlearned can reach the highest success in life. I mean by that, that a person who does not get into the habit of keeping the body clean, cannot do the highest work and the greatest amount of work in the world. When it comes to competing with persons who have learned the habit of keeping the body in good condition, you will find that the first named persons usually win in the race of life. I think many of you have already learned from your physiologies that when it comes to the combating of disease, where two persons are on a sick-bed with the same disease, the one who is habitually clean in his personal habits has a far greater chance for recovery than the one who has not learned the habit of cleanliness. You will also find that the person who is in the habit of caring for his body is in a better condition for study; he is in a condition to bear prolonged and severe exertion, while the person whose body is unclean is in a weak condition.

Take the matter of the teeth. Persons cannot call themselves educated and refined who do not make the matter of the cleanliness and proper care of their teeth an important part of themselves. When I speak of making such a thing a part of yourselves, I mean that you should make it such a strong habit that to leave it undone would seem unnatural. Some person has defined man as a bundle of habits. There are many habits that I wish you to make a part of yourselves, by practising so constantly that they may really be said to have become that.

There is the matter of the care of the hair, which everyone should make a part of himself. There is also the proper care of the finger nails.

Now all of these are common things, but they are great things. I should not recommend very highly a young man or young woman who went out from this institution as a graduate, and had not learned the habit of caring for the teeth, hair and nails systematically. Are you making these lessons a part of yourself?

Take the young men and young women who have been here two or three years. Have you grown to the point where you are dissatisfied and all out of sorts when your hair is not combed, your finger nails dirty, and your body not in the condition it should be in? If you have not reached that point, when you come to graduate, then there will be something wrong with your education, and you are not ready to go out from this institution, whether you are in the senior class or in the preparatory class.

Another thing; I confess that I cannot have the highest kind of respect for the person who is in the habit of going day after day with buttons off his clothes. There is no excuse for it, when buttons are so cheap. I wonder how many of you could stand, if I were now to ask all to stand who have every button in its place. I cannot have the best opinion of a girl who will let a hole remain in her apron day after day. Nor can I think well of a man who does not remove a grease spot from his coat as soon as he discovers it.

You have more respect for yourselves, and other people have more respect for you, when you get into the habit of polishing your shoes, no matter where you are, but especially when you are at school. Every man should get into the habit of polishing his shoes. See to it that they are in proper condition at all times.

BOOKER T. WASHINGTON

I need not repeat here, after what I have said, that it is of the utmost importance that every person wear the cleanest of linen. If I speak to you so plainly, it is because I want you to make these matters a part of yourselves to such an extent that they will be essential to your happiness and success. I want every girl who goes away from here to be so nearly perfect in her dress that she cannot be happy if there is any detail unattended to; and I want the same thing to be true of the young men. Let these things have an important bearing on your education here, and on your life hereafter.

And then, above all things, although on account of the number of students here you are very much crowded in your rooms and will have to make all the harder effort on that account, get into the habit of being orderly and neat. School your room-mates to the point where they will have a place for everything. Always know where to put your hands on anything you may want in your room, whether in the light or in the dark.

Then there are one or two other little things. You should have quiet in your rooms, at your work or in your talk with your fellow students. Do your work quietly. Get into the habit of closing doors quietly. You cannot realize how much all these little things add to your happiness and to the manhood and womanhood which you are going to build up as the years go on.

And then, in conclusion, so order your lives that you can form the habit of reading. Set aside a certain amount of time each day, even if it be not more than four or five minutes, for reading and studying aside from your lessons. Read books of travel, history and biography. I want you to patronize the library this year as never before. In it are great numbers of books by authors of the highest rank.

Be regular in all your habits. Have a regular time for studying, for recreation, and for sleeping.

And last, but far from least, set aside a regular time for thinking, for meditating with yourself. Take yourself up, pick yourself to pieces, see wherein you are weak and need strengthening. Analyze yourself. Get rid, as it were, of all the weights that have been holding you back, and resolve at the end of each week that you will walk upon your dead selves of the week before. If you will go on, making that kind of progress, you will find at the end of the nine school months that you are stronger in everything essential to good manhood and good womanhood.

To Would-be Teachers

S ince very many of you whom I see before me to-night will spend some part of your lives after you leave here as teachers, even if you do not make teaching your life work, I am going to talk over with you again a subject on which I have spoken elsewhere—How to build up a good school in the South.

The coloured schools of the South, especially in the country districts and smaller towns, are not kept open by the State fund, as a rule, longer than three or four months in the year. One of the great questions, then, with teachers and parents, is how to extend the school term to seven or eight months, so that the school shall really do some good.

I want to give a few plain suggestions, which will, I think, if carefully followed, result in placing a good school in almost every community. In this I am not speculating, because more than one Tuskegee graduate has built up a good school on the plan I outline.

In the first place the teacher must be willing to settle down in the community, and feel that that is to be his home, and teaching there his chief object in life while he is there. Not only must he not feel that he can move about from place to place every three months, but he must feel that he is not working for his salary alone. He must be willing to sacrifice for the good of the community.

The next thing is to get a convenient school-house. Usually, in the far South, the State has not been able to build a school-house. How is it to be secured? A good school-house should be carefully planned. Then the teacher or some one else should go among the people in the community, coloured and white, and get each individual to give something, no matter how small an amount if in money, or, if not in money, how little in value, for purchasing lumber. When we were getting started here at Tuskegee one old coloured woman brought me six eggs as her contribution to our work.

If enough money cannot be secured by subscription and collection to pay for the lumber, a supper, a festival, entertainment or church collection will help out. After the lumber is secured, the parents should be asked to "club in" with their waggons and haul it free. Then at least one good carpenter should be secured to take the lead in building. Each member of the community should agree to give a certain number of days' work in helping to put up the structure. In this work of building, the larger pupils can help a good deal, and they will have all the more interest in the school-house because they have had a hand in its erection. In these ways, by patient effort, a good frame school-house can be secured in almost any community.

Where it is possible, take a three or four months' public school as a starting point, and work in co-operation with the school officers, but do not let the school close at the end of these three or four months, because if that is done it will amount to almost nothing.

As soon as the teacher goes into a community, he should organize the people into an educational society or club, and there should be regular meetings once a week, or once in two weeks, at which plans for the improvement of the school should be discussed.

There are a number of ways for extending the school term. One is for each parent to pay ten, fifteen, twenty-five or fifty cents each month during the whole time the school is in session. Frequently parents who cannot pay in cash can let the teacher have eggs, chickens, butter, sweet potatoes, corn or some other kind of produce which will help to supply the teacher with food. Another plan is for each farmer to set aside a portion of land and give all that is raised upon it to the school. Still another plan, and one that is being successfully carried out in at least one place, and one that I think much of, is for the teacher to secure, either by renting or purchase, a small tract of land—say from two to five acres—and let the children cultivate this land while they are attending school. If, in this way, three bales of cotton can be raised, and a variety of vegetables and grain also, the produce can be sold and the school term extended from three months to six or seven months.

Some parents may object to this at first, but they will soon see that it is better to let the school close at one o'clock or two o'clock in the afternoon, so that the children may work on the school land for an hour or two, and in this way keep the school open six or seven months, than to let it close entirely at the end of three months. There is another advantage in this latter plan. The teacher can in this way teach the students, in a practical way, better methods of farming. Short talks on the principles of agriculture are worth much more to them than time spent in committing to memory the names of mountain peaks in Central Africa. Very often there is enough land right around the school-house for the pupils to cultivate.

In every case where it is possible, the teacher should buy a home in the community, and make his home in every way a model for those of the people who live around him. The teacher should cultivate a farm, or follow some trade while not teaching. This not only helps him, but sets a good example for the people in the community. If the teacher be a woman, there are few communities where she cannot add much to her income by sewing, dressmaking or poultry-raising.

The Cultivation of Stable Habits

I am going to speak with you a few minutes this evening upon the matter of stability. I want you to understand when you start out in school, that no individual can accomplish anything unless he means to stick to what he undertakes. No matter how many possessions he may have, no matter how much he may have in this or that direction, no matter how much learning or skill of hand he may possess, an individual cannot succeed unless, at the same time, he possesses that quality which will enable him to stick to what he undertakes. In a word he is not to be jumping from this thing to that thing.

That is the reason why so many ministers fail. They preach awhile, and then jump to something else. They do not stick to one thing. It is the same with many lawyers and doctors. They do not stick to what they undertake. Many business men fail for the same reason. When an individual gets a reputation—no matter what he has undertaken—of not having the quality of sticking to a thing until he succeeds in reaching the end, that reputation nullifies the influence for good of the better traits of his character in every direction. It is said of him that he is unstable.

I want you to begin your school life with the idea that you are going to stick to whatever you undertake until you have completed it. I take it for granted that all of you have come here with that idea in mind; that before you came here you sat down and talked the matter over with your father and mother, read over the circulars giving information about the school, and then deliberately decided that this institution was the one whose course of study you wished to complete. I take it for granted that you have come here with that end in view, and I want to say to you now, that you will injure yourselves, your parents, and the institution—and you will hurt your own reputation—unless, after having come here with the determination to succeed, you remain here for that purpose, and remain for the full time, until you receive your diploma. I hope every individual here, every young man and woman at the school, is here with the determination that he or she will not give up the struggle until the object aimed at has been attained.

You are at a stage now, when, if you begin jumping about here and there, if you begin in this course of study and then go to that course of study, you will very likely be jumping about from one thing to another all your life. You must make up your minds, after coming here, to do well whatever you undertake. This is a good rule not only to begin your school life with, but also to begin your later life with.

Perhaps I was never more interested than I was last evening in Montgomery, while standing on one of the streets there for an hour. I seldom stand on any street for an hour, but last night I did stand on that street for an hour, in front of a large, beautiful store that is owned by Mr. J. W. Adams, and watched the notice taken of the display of millinery made in his store windows by two girls that finished their academic and industrial courses at this school—Miss Jemmie Pierce and Miss Lydia Robinson. The first Monday in October is always the day in Montgomery for what they call the millinery openings; on that day the stores which handle such goods all make a great display of ladies' hats and bonnets. It was surprising and interesting to note how these two girls had entered a great city like Montgomery and had taken entire charge of the millinery department in a large store. Hundreds of people stopped to comment favourably upon the taste that was displayed in the decoration of those windows.

Now, all this work was done by two Tuskegee graduates. And the complimentary remarks that were made came not only from coloured people but from white people as well. No one could tell from the windows of that store whether it was a coloured or a white establishment. Many of the white ladies who were standing there did not know that they were standing in front of a store that was owned by a black man. It had none of the usual earmarks about it. Usually when you go into coloured establishments you see grease on the doors or on the counters; or you see this sign or that sign that this is a coloured man's establishment. Those of you here who are going to go into business after you leave school do not want to have any such earmarks about your establishments. Such a store as that of Mr. Adams is the kind of a store to have.

Now, these two young women have made a reputation for themselves. They went into the millinery division while they were here, and they remained until they graduated. One of them, I believe had not finished in the millinery department when she received her academic diploma, and so she came back last year and took a postgraduate course in millinery. It is interesting and encouraging to see these two young women succeeding in their work, and it all comes from their determination to succeed, and because they had sense enough to finish what they had undertaken.

That is the lesson that you all want to learn. If you do not learn it now, in a large degree you will be failures in life. You want to be like these young women. You want to fight it out. Now if you mean to get your diploma, you are going to have a hard time. Some of you are going to be without shoes, without a hat, without proper clothing of any kind. You will get discouraged because you have not as nice a dress or as nice a hat as this person or that person. I would not give a snap of my finger for a person who would give up for that. The thing for you to do is to fight it out. Get something in your head, and don't worry about what you can get to put on it. The clothes will come afterward.

You are going to be greatly discouraged sometimes, but if you will heed the lesson of fighting out what you have undertaken, that same disposition will follow you all through life, and you will get a reputation, because people will say of you that there is a person who sticks to whatever he or she undertakes. One of the saddest things in life is to see an individual who has grown to old age, with no profession, with no calling whatever from which he is sure of getting an independent living. It is sad to see such individuals without money, without homes, in their old age, simply because they did not learn the lesson of saving money and getting for themselves a beautiful home when they ought to have done this. And so, all through life, we can point to many people who have not learned this lesson—that for whatever they undertake they must pay the price which the world asks of them if they would succeed. If we are going to succeed we must pay the price for what we get; and he who accomplishes the most, accomplishes it in an humble and straightforward way, by sticking to what he has undertaken. He who does this finds in the end that he has achieved a tremendous success.

What you Ought to do

It is comparatively easy to perform almost any kind of work, but the value of any work is in having it performed so that the desired results may be most speedily reached, and in having the means with which the worker labours arranged so as to meet certain ends. It is the constant problem of those organs which have charge of the well-being of the body, to cause digestion to take place, so that what is nourishing in the food may reach every part of the body, not only the portions near the organs in which digestion takes place, but also the most extreme parts of the different members.

Just so it is the aim of all persons who are accustomed to making public addresses to try to make those who are far away from them hear them as well as those who sit near. In this same way, it seems to me more and more every year, it is going to be the main object of all our schools in the South to make their influence felt most forcibly among those who are remote from them. How can we reach the masses who are remote—I mean remote from educational advantages and from opportunities for encouragement and enlightenment? The problem in the rural districts is difficult because of the vastness of the number to be reached, and of the frequent difficulty of reaching them. We must keep this fact before us, then; that institutions of this kind are of little value unless they can pave the way to make the results of their work felt among the masses of the people who are especially remote from these institutions.

It is a fact, as most of you know, that we very seldom meet with a thoroughly well-educated teacher in the rural districts, in spite of the passing of over thirty years since we became men and women. You know, too, that the same thing is, in too large a measure, true of the ministry. The responsibility for reaching these people, for affecting them for good, rests upon the young men and young women who are being educated in these Southern institutions to-day.

What are you going to do as your part towards reaching these people, towards carrying to them the light which they need so much and so earnestly long for? Difficult as this problem is, it is not a discouraging one, because these people are ready to follow the light as soon as they are sure that the right kind of light is set up before them. You very seldom meet with a coloured man who is not conscious of his ignorance, and who is not anxious to get up as soon as he finds himself down. In this respect the problem is encouraging.

One of the ways in which the problem is serious is with respect to labour. In almost every city and town in the South a large proportion of the coloured people are shiftless so far as manual labour is concerned, although I think there is already improvement. The masses of our people are given to thrift and industry, and to unremitting toil, in their way. The hard thing about it, the discouraging thing, is that they do not know how to realize on the results of their toil; because they have no education and little idea of industrial development, they do not know how to make their work tell for what it ought to. As a general thing the people—those in the country especially—do not ask anybody to come and give them food, clothing and houses; all they ask is for some person, some honest, upright man or woman who is interested in their welfare, to come among them and show them how to direct their efforts and their energy, show them how best to realize on the results of their work, so that they can supply their own moral, religious and material needs and educate their children.

And you will find that wherever this institution, Hampton, Talladega, Fisk, Atlanta or any other, can put in the midst of the people young men and young women who will settle down among them and make their lives object lessons for the people—plant a good school and convince the people that the teacher has settled down there to stay through encouraging or discouraging circumstances—you will find that such a teacher will not only be encouraged, but will be supported materially. In every way there will be an opportunity for that person to revolutionize the community. That opportunity is open to you. It is an opportunity which is being opened to no other set of young men and young women who are being educated anywhere else in the world. Are you going to appreciate the beauty and grandeur of this opportunity?

I was talking with a gentleman last night who has recently spent some time in one of the Southern states, and he told me that in hardly any country district in that state was there a public school which is kept open longer than four months. He tells me that the average salary in some of those districts is little more than fifteen dollars a month. In another state the condition of the people is about the same. In our own state perhaps the conditions are worse even than in the states referred to. In some counties in Alabama the people are this year receiving no money to run their schools more than three and a half months in the year, except, of course, in the cities and towns. In some counties the teachers are being paid only twelve to twenty dollars, and there are possibly some where the teachers get not more than ten dollars from the state fund.

I was talking with a gentleman from another state not long ago about the material condition of the people in that state, and he told me that so far as their industrial life is concerned, the masses are in a very bad condition this year; that they are too often at the mercy of the landowners—I refer to the persons who run the large plantations—and that the same thing is largely true of all of the cotton-raising states. I need not go on to describe to you the moral results that must inevitably follow such a condition of things. I need not take your time to tell you that there can be little morality or religion among people who are so ignorant as these people, and who do not know where they are going to get anything to eat. It is needless to describe the train of moral evils that must follow such conditions as these.

What I have attempted to describe to you as existing to-day in these country districts may not be very encouraging, but it seems to me that every young man and young woman who has enjoyed the privileges afforded by this and by other institutions in the South—I speak especially now to the members of the next graduating class—should feel that such conditions as these present one of the most inviting fields possible for labour. Every young man and woman here is being educated by money that is given by others. None of you are paying for the education you are receiving. You might pay for your board, but you would have to do that elsewhere. Every one must pay for his or her own clothing, but the cost of buildings, rent, tuition, expenses and other matters pertaining to the institution you do not pay. Your education, in a large measure, is a gift from the public, and it seems to me that one of the first things you should do is to repay, to as large an extent as is possible with your services, what has been spent in giving you so large a part of your education.

This is a debt that you owe not only to yourselves, but to our race and our country. It is a religious debt as well, that you be willing to go out into these country districts and suffer, as it were, for a few years, until you can get a foothold, so that you can plant yourselves in one of these dark communities. I feel sure that you would not have to suffer very long. I believe that the hardest part of the struggle would come during the first two or three years. When you can convince the people that you

BOOKER T. WASHINGTON

are in earnest, the battle is won. When you can convince them that it is cheaper to keep an educated teacher than to keep one who is ignorant, and when you can once demonstrate your value to them not only in an educational respect but industrially and morally, the battle is won, and these people will stand by you and support you. In many cases, it is my belief, you will eventually find yourselves better supported financially than you would if you had gone to work in cities and large towns. No matter from which side you look at this problem, good is bound to come from it.

And while we are talking about the reward that will come as a result of your services, let me tell you that no greater satisfaction can come to any one than that which you will get from the worship and praise which will come to you from these old mothers and fathers who will be benefited by your services. I know of instances where teachers have gone and planted themselves in these country districts who, even if they do not make such a very great success financially, receive the love and most sincere worship from year to year, because of the feeling of gratitude which the people among whom they have settled have for them on account of their having helped them in so many ways.

This same kind of pioneer work had to be done all over the world before the right kind of civilization was planted. It was such work as this that the people did who settled the great West, where they were deprived of the comforts of life. The people who planted Oberlin College in what was then a wilderness had to suffer many such hardships. The men who went to Washington, Oregon, and California and established what are now large cities there, had to suffer many such hardships; they had to suffer just what you must and should suffer. Are you going to suffer for your own people until they can receive the light which they so much need? If the young men and women before me have the right kind of stuff in them they will do this. Most certainly do I hope that you are going to carry out into these dark communities the light which you receive here from day to day. I hope you will fill these districts with men and women of education. When you go out from here with your diploma, whether it be next May or at some other time, resolve to plant yourself in one community and stay there. No matter what your work is, you cannot accomplish much if you become the wandering Jew. Find the community where you think you can use your life to the best advantage, and then stay there.

(In the time that has elapsed since this talk was given, I think there has been improvement in many of the country schools in the South, and in the general condition of the people as described to me then.—B. T. W.)

INDIVIDUAL RESPONSIBILITY

I have referred in a general way, before this, when I have been speaking to you, to the fact that each one of you ought to feel an interest in whatever task is set you to do here over and above the mere bearing which that task has on your own life. I wish to speak more specifically to-night on this subject—on what I may term the importance of your feeling a sense of personal responsibility not only for the successful performance of every task set you, but for the successful outcome of every worthy undertaking with which you come in contact.

You ought to realize that your actions will not affect yourselves alone. In this age it is almost impossible for a man to live for himself alone. On every side our lives touch those of others; their lives touch ours. Even if it were possible to live otherwise, few would wish to. A narrow life, a selfish life, is almost sure to be not only unprofitable but unhappy. The happy people and the successful people are those who go out of their way to reach and influence for good as many persons as they can. In order to do this, though, in order best to fit one's self to live this kind of life, it is important that certain habits be acquired; and an essential one of these is the habit of realizing one's responsibility to others.

Your actions will affect other people in one way or another, and you will be responsible for the result. You ought always to remember this, and govern yourselves accordingly. Suppose it is the matter of the recitation of a lesson, for instance. Some one may say: "It is nobody's business but my own if I fail in a recitation. Nobody will suffer but me." This is not so. Indirectly you injure your teacher also, for while a conscientious, hard-working teacher ought not to be blamed for the failures of pupils who do not learn simply because they do not want to, or are too lazy to try, it is generally the case that a teacher's reputation gains or loses as his or her class averages high or low. And each failure in recitation, for whatever cause, brings down the average. Then, too, you are having an influence upon your classmates, even if it be unconscious. There is hardly ever a student who is not observed by some one at some time as an example. "There is such a boy," some other student says to himself. "He has failed in class ever so many times, and still he gets along. It can't make much difference if I fail once." And as a result he neglects his duty, and does fail.

The same thing is true of work in the industrial departments. Too many students try to see how easily they can get through the day, or the work period, and yet not get into trouble. Or even if they take more interest than this, they care for their work only for the sake of what they can get out of it for themselves, either as pay, or as instruction which will enable them to work for pay at some later time. Now there ought to be a higher impulse behind your efforts than that. Each student ought to feel that he or she has a personal responsibility to do each task in the very best manner possible. You owe this not only to your fellow-students, your teachers, the school, and the people who support the institution, but you owe it even more to yourselves. You owe it to yourselves because it is right and honest, because nothing less than this is right and honest, and because you never can be really successful and really happy until you do study and work and live in this way.

I have been led to speak specifically on this subject to-night on account of two occurrences here which have come to my notice. One of these illustrates the failure on the part of students to feel this sense of responsibility to which I have referred. The other affords an illustration of the possession by a student of a feeling of personal interest and personal responsibility which has been very gratifying and encouraging. The first incident, I may say, occurred some months ago. It is possible that the students who were concerned in it may not be here now or, if they are, that it would not happen again. I certainly hope not.

A gentleman who had been visiting here was to go away. He left word at the office of his wish, saying that he planned to leave town on the five o'clock train in the afternoon. A boy was sent from the office early in the afternoon with a note to the barn ordering a carriage to take this gentleman and his luggage to the station. Half-past four came, and the man had his luggage brought down to the door of the building in which he had been staying, so as to be ready when the team came. But no team came. The visitor finally became so anxious that he walked over to the barn himself. Just as he reached the barn he met the man who was in charge there, with the note in his hand. The note had only just that moment reached this man, and of course no carriage had been sent because the first person who felt that he had any responsibility in the matter had only just learned that a carriage was wanted. The boy who had brought the note had given it to another boy, and he to someone else, and he, perhaps, to someone else. At any rate it had been delayed because no one had taken enough interest in the errand to see that whatever business the note referred to received proper attention. This occurred, as I have said, several months ago, before the local train here went over to Chehaw to meet all of the trains. It happened that this particular passenger was going north, and it was possible by driving to Chehaw for him to get there in time to take the north-bound train. If he had been going the other way, though, towards Montgomery, he would have lost the train entirely, and, as chanced to be the case, would have been unable to keep a very important engagement. As it was, he was obliged to ride to Chehaw in a carriage, and the time of a man and team, which otherwise would have been saved, was required to take him there.

Now when such a thing as this happens, no amount of saying, "I am sorry," by the person or persons to blame, will help the matter any. It is too late to help it then. The thing to do is to feel some responsibility in seeing that things are done right yourself. Take enough interest in whatever you are engaged in to see that it is going to come out in the end just as nearly right, just as nearly perfect, as anything you can do will go towards making it right or perfect. And if the task or errand passes out of your hands before it is completed, do not feel that your responsibility in the matter ends until you have impressed it upon the minds and heart of the person to whom you turn over the further performance of the duty.

The world is looking for men and women who can tell one why they can do this thing or that thing, how a certain difficulty was surmounted or a certain obstacle removed. But the world has little patience with the man or woman who takes no real interest in the performance of a duty, or who runs against a snag and gets discouraged, and then simply tells why he did not do a thing, and gives excuses instead of results. Opportunities never come a second time, nor do they wait for our leisure. The years come to us but once, and they come then only to pass swiftly on, bearing the ineffaceable record we have put upon them. If we wish to make them beautiful years or profitable years, we must do it moment by moment as they glide before us.

The other case to which I have referred is pleasanter to speak about. One day this spring, after it had got late enough in the season so that it was not as a general thing necessary to have fires to heat our buildings, a student passing Phelps Hall noticed that there was a volume of black smoke pouring out of one of the chimneys there. Some boys might not have noticed the smoke at all; others would have said that it came from the chimney; still others would have said that it was none of their business anyway, and would have gone along. This boy was different. He noticed the smoke, and although he saw, or thought he saw that it came from the chimney, and if so was probably no sign of harm, he felt that any smoke at all there at that time was such an unusual thing that it ought to be investigated for fear it might mean danger to the building. He was not satisfied until he had gone into the building and had inspected every floor clear up to the attic, to see that the chimney and the building were not in danger. As it happened, the janitor had built a fire in the furnace in the basement for some reason, so that the young man's anxiety fortunately was unfounded, but I am heartily glad he had such an anxiety, and that he could not rest until he found out whether there was any foundation for it or not. I shall feel that all of our buildings are safer for his being here, and when he graduates and goes away I hope he will leave many others here who will have the same sense of personal responsibility which he had. Let me tell you, here and now, that unless you young men and young women come to have this characteristic, your lives are going to fall far short of the best and noblest achievement possible.

We frequently hear the word "lucky" used with reference to a man's life. Two boys start out in the world at the same time, having the same amount of education. When twenty years have passed, we find one of them wealthy and independent; we find him a successful professional man with an assured reputation, or perhaps at the head of a large commercial establishment employing many men, or perhaps a farmer owning and cultivating hundreds of acres of land. We find the second boy, grown now to be a man, working for perhaps a dollar or a dollar and a half a day, and living from hand to mouth in a rented house. When we remember that the boys started out in life equal-handed, we may be tempted to remark that the first boy has been fortunate, that fortune has smiled on him; and that the second has been unfortunate. There is no such nonsense as that. When the first boy saw a thing that he knew he ought to do, he did it; and he kept rising from one position to another until he became independent. The second boy was an eye-servant who was afraid that he would do more than he was paid to do—he was afraid that he would give fifty cents' worth of labour for twenty-five cents. He watched the clock, for fear that he would work one minute past twelve o'clock at noon and past six o'clock at night. He did not feel that he had any responsibility to look out for his employer's interests. The first boy did a dollar's worth of work for fifty cents. He was always ready to be at the store before time; and then, when the bell rang to stop work, he would go to his employer and ask him if there was not something more that ought to be done that night before he went home. It was this quality in the first boy that made him valuable and caused him to rise. Why should we call him "fortunate" or "lucky?" I think it would be much more suitable to say of him: "He is responsible."

Getting on in the World

It is natural and praiseworthy for a person to be looking for a higher and better position than the one he occupies. So long as a man does his whole duty in what he is engaged in, he is not to be condemned for looking for something better to do. Now the question arises:—How are you going to put yourself in a condition to be in demand for these higher and more important positions?

In the first place you should be continually on the lookout for opportunities to improve yourselves in your present work. You should be constantly on the lookout for chances to make yourselves more valuable to your present employer, and more efficient in your work for him. Suppose you are engaged in the work of milking cows—I think it better to talk of practical things with which you all are acquainted, although I know that many of you boys had rather I would tell you how to go to Congress than how to become successful milkers. Inasmuch, though, as I suspect a good many more of us will have to milk cows than can go to Congress, I think it will not hurt us to talk about milking. If the boy who milks cows now does that thoroughly, by doing it he may lay the foundation to go to Congress later. The point is, that we want to be constantly on the lookout for ways of improving whatever work we are engaged in, whether that work be milking cows or doing something else.

In whatever you are doing, there are a great many improvements which you want to become acquainted with. If your work is dairying, read the dairy journals. Get hold of every book or paper that you can which has anything to do with your line of work. Be sure that you know all—or as nearly as possible all—there is to be known about milking cows. And then don't be content with what you get out of books and newspapers, for that information is only the result of some other person's experience. By conversing with intelligent and experienced persons, and by your own experiments, you can get much valuable information about your work. Never get to the point where you are ashamed to ask somebody else for information. The ignorant man will always be ignorant, if he fears that by asking for information he will betray his lack of knowledge.

Know all there is to be known about the position you occupy, but ever feel that there is more for you to learn. There is no person who makes himself of so little use in the world as the one who feels that he knows all there is to be known about his work. If you are milking cows, and feel that you know all there is to be known about that subject, you have simply reached a point where you are practically useless and unfitted for the work. Feel that you can always learn something from somebody else. It is a mark of intelligence to learn, even from the humblest person. I do not mean for you always to put into practice every suggestion that is made to you, or to agree with every statement made to you; but listen to what people say, weigh their plans alongside of your own, and then profit by the one which you are convinced is the best. Persevere in such conversation, and in reading. You will constantly be surprised to find how little you really know about your work, and how much more somebody else knows about it than you do.

You want to get to the point where you can anticipate the wants of your employer. In this way you will make yourself of great service to him. You do not know how vexing and discouraging it is to a man to be compelled to say every morning to those in his employ: "Do this at nine o'clock, and that at twelve o'clock, and the other at five;" or how pleasant it is to have a person with whom you come in contact anticipate the needs of the man who employs him.

Then you can make yourself valuable and in demand just in proportion as you consider that the work you are performing is your own. Do not consider that it is being performed for a certain man or a particular organization. Make haste and get to the point where you can feel that everything connected with the shop in which you work, or in the office, or in the stable, is under your care, and that you alone are responsible for it. If you are at the head of a stable or barn, plan day by day how you can best provide for the well-being of your cows and horses. When you make yourself master of these humble positions, you will find that the calls to higher places will come to you. The men you see spending most of their time looking for higher and more lucrative positions are, nine times out of ten, men who have made worthless failures in other places.

Each One His Part

I desire to call your attention for a few minutes to-night to the fact that one thing is dependent for success upon another, one individual is dependent for success upon another, one family in a community upon other families for their mutual prosperity, one part of a State upon the other parts for the successful government of the State. The same thing is true in nature. One thing cannot exist unless another exists; cannot succeed without the success of something else. The very forces of nature are dependent upon other forces for their existence. Without vegetable life we could not have animal life; without mineral life we could not have vegetable life. So, throughout all kinds of life, as throughout the life of nature, everything is dependent upon something else for its success.

The same thing is true of this institution and of every institution. The success of the whole depends upon having every person connected with the institution do his or her whole duty.

We are very apt to get the idea that there are high positions and that there are low positions, that there is important service and unimportant service; but I believe that God expects the same amount of conscientious work from a person in a low position as from one in a high position, that He expects the same conscientious service whether the work be a big task or a little one. We are dependent as an institution—every institution is dependent—for success, upon the individual consciences of those connected with it as teachers and students; and there is nothing that gives me more satisfaction and pleasure, and more faith in the future of the school, than to see examples of conscientious work here.

I remember a special instance of this kind that occurred at one of our Commencements. I believe that Commencement, more than any other time in the school year, is an occasion when there is excitement and a desire to witness the exercises. After the exercises of that year were over, I had occasion to go to the dining room, and I found there one of the teachers who from her appearance I thought had not attended the exercises. When I asked her about this, she said: "No. I intended to go, but at the last minute I saw that there were some dishes here that needed to be washed, and I stayed here to see that they were washed."

Now that was one of the finest exhibitions of conscientious regard for duty that I ever saw, and there are very few persons who would have done a thing like that. That we have teachers here whose hearts are so much in their work that they are willing to do such things as this gives me great faith in the future of this school as the years go on.

It takes a person with a conscience, when there are public men of note here, a great many strangers and many things to attract attention, to be so mindful of her duty that she will stay behind and wash dishes when every one else is in attendance upon the exercises and seeking enjoyment. When the people connected with this institution can bring themselves up to that point, I have no fear for the success of the institution; and it can succeed only as they do bring their consciences up to that point.

If I were to ask you individually as students to deliver an address upon this platform, or to read an essay, I should not be at all afraid that you would fail. I believe that you would carefully prepare that address or essay. You would look up all the references necessary in order to give you what information you needed, and then you would get up here and speak or read successfully. I feel sure that I would hear something that I should not be ashamed of. The average man and woman does succeed when before the public. But where I fear for your success is when you come to the performance of the small duties—the duties which you think no one else will know about, the things which no one will see you do. It is when you think that no one is going to see you washing dishes, or getting dirt out of crevices, that I am afraid you are going to fail.

I remember that some time ago when I was travelling in a buggy from one New England village to another, after we had gone some miles on our way, the young man who was driving me stopped the horse and got out. I asked him what was the matter, and he said that something was the matter with the harness. I looked with all the eyes I had, and yet I could see nothing at fault. Still the man mended a piece of harness that he said was not as it should be. It had not seemed to me that this fault in the harness had been irritating the horse or hindering him from going so fast as he ought, but after it had been repaired I could see a difference for the better. That, to my mind, was a great lesson. It taught me how the people of New England have educated their consciences so that they cannot allow themselves to let even the smallest thing go undone or be improperly done. It is this trait in the New England character that has come to make the very name itself of that part of the country a synonym for success. Don't we wish that we had a hundred such men as that driver here! If I could put my hand on a thousand such persons as that, we could find employment for all of them as soon as they got their diplomas.

One learns to judge persons by their character in this respect. Not long ago I had an opportunity to go through the jail of this county. As the sheriff showed me through the building I was impressed to see how clean everything was, and I noticed that the man who seemed to be the janitor of the jail, although he too was a prisoner, seemed to take a great deal of pride in showing me the cleanness of the corners and the general good appearance of the place. He seemed to put his whole heart into the keeping of that jail clean.

"Who is that man?" I asked the sheriff, after we had got out of the janitor's hearing.

"He is a prisoner," the sheriff replied, "but I believe he is innocent. I do not believe that a man can be so honest and faithful about his work and be guilty of a crime. When I see how well he does his work here, notwithstanding the fact that he is shut up here in prison, I believe that he is an honest man and deserves his freedom."

In plain words, then, the problem we must work out here is not:—Can you master algebra, or literature? We know you can do that. We know you can master the sciences. The general problem we have to work out here, and work it out with fear and trembling, is:—Can we educate the individual conscience? Can we so educate a group of students that there will be in every one of them a conscience on which we can depend. Can we educate a class of girls here who will not be satisfied when sweeping their rooms to make the middle of the rooms look clean, but leave a trail of dirt in the corners and under the furniture? Will they see to it that everything is properly cleaned and put in its appropriate place? Can we educate a class of young men who will do their duty on the farm as they would do it on this platform? Can we educate your consciences so that you will do certain things, not because it is the rule that they should be done, but because they should be done? These are the problems we must work out here.

What Would Father and Mother Say?

I think there is no more important or more critical time in a person's life than when he or she leaves home for the first time, to enter school, or to go to work, or to go into business. I think that as a general thing you can judge pretty accurately what a person is going to amount to in life by the way he or she acts during the first year or two after leaving home.

You will find, usually, that if a young man is able during this time to stand up against temptation, is able to practise the lessons that his father and mother have taught him, and instead of falling by the wayside gains help and inspiration as he goes along from these lessons, he is almost sure to prove himself a valuable citizen, one who not only will be a help to his parents in their old age, but a help to the community in which he lives.

There is no better way to test an act than to ask yourself the question: "What would my father or my mother think of this? Would they approve, or should I be ashamed to let them know that I have done this thing?" If you will ask yourselves these questions day by day, I think you will find that you will get a great deal of assistance from them in the shaping of your lives while you are here at school.

I want you to put that question to yourselves with regard to deportment, because that is a thing on which we must lay emphasis. We can fill your heads with knowledge, and we can train your hands to work with skill, but unless all this training of head and hand is based upon high, upright character, upon a true heart, it will amount to nothing. You will be no better off than the most ignorant.

Now, one of the ways in which young people are likely to go astray, especially when they first go away from home to school, is in yielding to a temptation to spend their time with persons who have mean and low dispositions; persons whom you would be ashamed to have your parents know that you kept company with. Avoid that. Be sure that the young men and women with whom you associate are persons who are able to raise you up, persons who will help to make you stronger in every way.

I do not need to tell you, I am sure, of the consequences of association with persons who will have, a bad influence upon you, or the results of a disregard of admonitions for good. A student who persistently keeps bad company, who breaks rules, who is constantly disobedient, who is repeatedly behind at roll call, who time after time has to be called up by the officer of the day, or watched in the dining room or on the parade ground, is the student who in a few years is going to bring sorrow to the hearts of his parents. There is no getting away from that.

Only to-day the mother of one of the students came here with a message from another mother whose son had been sent here. She told me how this anxious mother had told her to impress upon her son the necessity of obeying every rule here, and how she wanted him to put in every moment in hard study and honest work. She wanted this woman to impress upon the boy how hard his mother was struggling every day so that she could keep him here, and at the same time provide for the younger children of the family at home. Now, when this message was delivered, where was that boy? Was he doing as his mother was so earnestly praying him to do? No. He had already disgraced himself, and had been sent away from the institution. How much sorrow will he bring to his poor mother's heart when she knows! No wonder he was trying to conceal his misconduct and disgrace from her.

Let me entreat you, then, if you are inclined to fritter away the best hours of your lives, think how the news of your misconduct will act upon the hearts of your parents, those fathers and mothers whose every thought is of you.

I have spoken of these as some of the things that we do not want to have you do at school. What are some of the things that we do want you to learn to do? We want to have you learn to see and appreciate the practical value of the religion of Christ. We hope to help you to see that religion, that Christianity, is not something that is far off, something in the air, that it is not something to be enjoyed only after the breath has left the body. We want to have you see that the religion of Christ is a real and helpful thing; that it is something which you can take with you into your class-rooms, into your shops, on to the farm, into your very sleeping rooms, and that you do not have to wait until to-morrow before you can find out about the power and helpfulness of Christ's religion.

We want to have you feel that this religion is a part of your lives, and that it is meant to be a help to you from day to day. We hope to have you feel that the religious services that we have you attend here are not burdens, but that it is a privilege, greatly to be desired, to come to these meetings, and into the prayer meetings of the various societies on the grounds, and there commune, not in a far-off, imaginary way, but in an humble but intimate way, with the spirit of Jesus. We want you to feel that religion is something to make you happier, brighter and more hopeful, not something to make you go about with long, solemn faces. We want you to learn, if you do not already know, that in order to be Christlike one does not have to be unnatural.

Then we want to have you to learn to govern your actions, not alone for the sake of the result which they will have upon yourself and those who are near and dear to you, but for the sake of your influence upon all with whom you will come in contact. Your life here will be largely wasted—I am tempted to say wholly wasted—if you fail to learn that higher, broader, and far more important lesson of your relations to your fellow-students and to all the persons by whom you are going to be daily surrounded. Your life will be wasted if you go away from here and have not learned that the greatest lesson of all is the lesson of brotherly love, of usefulness and of charity. I want to see young men who are here realize this spirit to such an extent that they will rise in chapel and give their seats to students who are strangers at the school. I want to have you get to the point where you will go to the matron in the dining room and ask her permission to have some new student who has not had a chance to get acquainted take his meals at a seat beside you.

Of the many noble traits exhibited by the late General Armstrong, none made a deeper impression upon me than his supreme unselfishness. I do not believe that I ever saw in all my association with General Armstrong anything in his life or actions which indicated in the slightest degree that he was selfish. He was interested not only in the black South, but in the white South, not only in his own school, but in all schools. Anything which he could do or say to benefit another institution seemed to give him as much pleasure as if he were speaking or acting directly for the benefit of Hampton Institute.

I had a pleasant experience of this spirit of a desire to be helpful to others a little while ago, when I was visiting a certain theological seminary in Pennsylvania. I think I was never in such an atmosphere as during the two days I spent in that institution. I was surrounded by a crowd of young men whose sole object seemed to be to make me comfortable and happy. Most of these young men were far advanced in the study of theology and the sciences, and yet they were not above serving me, even to the extent of offering to black my boots. When I came away several wished to carry my luggage to the station. This is the kind of thoughtfulness we want to have in every corner of this institution. Get hold of the spirit of wanting to help somebody else. Seek every opportunity possible to make somebody happy and comfortable. Do all this, and you will find that the years will not be many before we will have one of the best institutions on the face of the globe, and that you, in helping to make it such, have been doing things that, when you ask yourselves: "What would father and mother say about my doing this?" will enable you to answer the question with pride and satisfaction.

Object Lessons

N ot long ago an old coloured man living in this State said to me: "I's done quit libin' in de ashes. I's got my second freedom."

That remark meant, in this case, that that old man by economy, hard work and proper guidance, after twenty years of struggle, had freed himself from debt, had paid for fifty acres of land, had built a comfortable house, and was a tax-payer. It meant that his two sons had been educated in academic and agricultural branches, that his daughter had received mental training in connection with lessons in sewing and cooking. Within certain limitations here was a Christian, American home, the result of industrial effort and philanthropy. This Negro had been given a chance to get upon his feet. That is all that any Negro in America asks. That is all that you in this school ask.

What position in State, in letters, or in commerce and in business the offspring of that man is to occupy must be left to the future and the capacity of the race. What position you are to occupy must be left to your future and to your capacity. During the days of slavery we were shielded from competition. To-day, unless we prepare ourselves to compete with the world, we must go to the wall as a race.

If I were to go into certain communities in the United States and say that the German is ignorant, I should be pointed to the best-paying truck-farm in that neighbourhood, owned and operated by a German. If I said that the German is without skill, I should be shown the largest machine-shop in the city, owned and operated by a German. If I said the German is lazy, I should be shown the largest and finest residence on the most fashionable avenue, built from the savings of a German who began life in poverty. If I said that the German could not be trusted, I should be introduced to a man of that race who is the president of the largest bank in the city. If I said that the German is not fitted for citizenship, I should be shown a German who is a respected and influential member of the city government.

Now, when your critics say that the Negro is lazy, I want you to be able to show them the finest farm in the community owned and operated by a Negro. When they ask if the Negro is honest, I want you to show them a Negro whose note is acceptable at the bank for $5,000. When they say that the Negro is not economical, I want you to show them a Negro with $50,000 in the bank. When they say that the Negro is not fit for citizenship, I want you to show them a man of our race paying taxes on a cotton factory. I want you to be able to show them Negroes who stand in the front in the affairs of State, of religion, of education, of mechanics, of commerce and of household economy. You remember the old admonition: "By this sign we shall conquer." Let it be our motto.

There are people in the North who have been aiding in the matter of Negro education in the South during the last ten, twenty, or even thirty years. It is in part the money of those people that has made this institution possible. Those people have a right, as a plain matter of business, to ask what are the results of this aid they have been giving. What evidences can we present to prove to them that their investments in this direction have been paying ones? It is, in no small measure, the duty of you, as students of Tuskegee Institute, to answer, and to answer satisfactorily, such a question as that.

We have reached a point, largely through the aid which the North has given to the South during the last thirty years, where there is little opposition in the South to the people of the Negro race receiving any form of education. You can go out from here and plant a school in any county in the South, which will not meet with opposition from the white residents of the community. What is more, in many cases it will receive encouragement, and in some a hearty sympathy and support. Not long ago I received fifty dollars from a white man in Mississippi to pay for the education of a black boy. This man was formerly a slave-holder, and at first he was not inclined to encourage the education of the Negro, but he stated to me frankly, in his letter, that he now believes that Tuskegee and similar institutions are doing the work that the Negro most needs to have done. He wanted to show the people of the North, he said, that Southern white men are as deeply interested in the development of the Negro as they are. I have in mind another case, of a Southern white man in Alabama who during the last year contributed out of his own pocket nearly $2,000 for the building and maintenance of a Negro school in his county. Still another Southern white man, Mr. Belton Gilreath, of Birmingham, Alabama, recently sent the Institute his check for $500—up to that time the largest sum which the school had received from a Southern man—with this letter:

"As a Southern man and the son of one of the largest slave owners of the South, I am anxious for our people to do all that can reasonably be expected of them for the education of the Negroes, thereby making them more content and useful citizens and friends.

BOOKER T. WASHINGTON

"Furthermore, I think the time has come in the South for all our people to consider more fully than they have ever done before the question of the education of *all of our population*; and, wherever practicable, to give attention in our schools to teaching the art of saving also."

More recently still, Mr. H. M. Atkinson, of Atlanta, one of the most successful business men in the entire South, came to Tuskegee Institute and made a thorough inspection of our work. After he returned to Atlanta I received a letter from him from which I quote one paragraph: "I enclose my check for $1,000, for the benefit of your school, to be used as your judgment dictates. I was very much impressed by what I saw. I will not forget it."

These white people are beginning to see the difference between the value of an educated Negro and one who is not educated. It is for you to demonstrate to them this value more and more clearly every year.

Substance vs. Shadow

You are here for the purpose of getting an education. Now, one of the results of an education is to increase a person's wants. You take the ordinary person who lives on a plantation, and so long as that person is ignorant, he is content to live in a cabin with one room, in which he has a skillet, a bedstead—or an apology for one—a table, and a few chairs or stools. He is content if he has fat meat, corn bread and peas on the table to eat, and for clothing he is satisfied to wear jeans and osnaburg himself, and to have his wife wear a calico dress and a twenty-five cent hat.

But, as soon as that man becomes educated, he feels that he must have a house with at least two or three rooms in it, furnished with neat and substantial furniture. Instead of jeans and osnaburg for clothes, he wants decent woollen cloth, neat-fitting shoes, and a white collar and a necktie, things which he never thought of wearing before he became educated. Sometimes he even thinks that he must have jewellery.

So you see the result of education is to increase a person's wants. Now, the crisis in that person's affairs comes when the question arises whether his education has increased his ability to supply his wants. Such an ability, I claim, is one of the results of industrial education. By such an education as that, while we are getting culture along all the lines that in any degree tend to increase the wants of a person, we are, in the meantime, getting skill to increase our ability to supply these wants. And, unless we have this ability, we will find, sooner or later, that instead of going forward we are going backward.

I think that the temptation for us, especially for those who are only half educated, is to try to get hold of a certain kind of shallow culture, instead of getting the substantial—instead of getting hold of real education, of property and material prosperity.

You who study history know how the Pilgrim Fathers, who landed at Plymouth Rock in the bleak winter of 1620, were willing to wear homespun clothes, and to be married in them, if necessary, and to have a wedding that in all would not cost more than four dollars, I suppose. On the other hand, when one of our boys wants to get married now, he must have a wedding that costs not less than one hundred and fifty dollars. His wife must have a dress with a long train, and he must have a Prince Albert, broadcloth coat that he either rents, or buys on the instalment plan. They think that they must have a bevy of waiting bridesmaids, and there must be a line of hacks standing on the outside of the church door that will cost him not less than twenty-five dollars. Then, after the ceremony, where do these people go to live? The chances are the young man who has been to all this expense for the sake of the show of it, takes his bride to live in a small cabin with only two rooms— sometimes only one room—rented at that.

This is what I mean by getting the superficial culture before the dollars are made; grasping at the shadow instead of the substance. Now what we want to do here is to send out a set of young men and young women who will go into the communities where such mistakes as these are made, and show the people by example and by work how much better it is to get married for four dollars, and to pay as you go, than to get married for a hundred and fifty dollars, and then pay four dollars a month to live in a rented cabin. When I go to New York, or to any large city, there is nothing more discouraging than to see people of this very class I am speaking of, people who seek the superficial culture, the shadow, rather than the substantial dollars and education. If you stand for a few minutes on any of the fashionable streets in the Northern cities, you will see these elaborately dressed men, wearing five dollar hats on heads that at most are not worth more than fifty cents. This is the class of people who have got just enough education to make them want everything they see, but who have not got enough to make them able to get what they want unless they go beyond their means to do so.

A superficial education, too, makes us inclined to seek show in other things besides dress. We are inclined, for one thing, to seek to show off in the use of titles. I remember that once I was introduced to a company of about sixty men, and out of the whole number there were only six who were not doctors, professors, or colonels, or who did not have some title. I must say I thought more of the six who were just plain misters than I did of all the rest, for among the others there were some very hard-looking doctors and professors. An over-desire for these things shows a shallowness in us which makes us ridiculous. We want to stop making that kind of mistake. If you are a mister, encourage the people to call you by that title. If you are a minister and preach interesting and instructive sermons, people are going to be impressed by what you say and not by the title you bear. The title is the shadow; what you say is the substance.

When a person is simple, he is on the strong side. People not only have more respect for him, but he accomplishes more. I was once at a memorial meeting held in honour of a man who had done a great and useful work, not only for the race but for the school with which he had been connected. After about two hours of speechmaking, somebody took the platform and said that a collection ought to be taken up for the benefit of the school which this man had worked so hard for, to show the appreciation which those present felt for this man's services. After a good deal of talk, $6.65 was collected. Then the question was raised again as to what was going to be done with this money—just how it was to be donated to the school.

The meeting had passed a set of resolutions testifying to the high character of the man and the worth of his work. Somebody suggested that these resolutions be engrossed and sent to the school. This was a big word, and the people liked the sound of it. Upon inquiry it was found that it would cost $6.00 to have the resolutions engrossed. It was voted to have this done, and it was done; when the resolutions would have done just as much good typewritten, at a cost of twenty-five cents. But the meeting paid out the $6.00, and sent the engrossed copy of the resolutions down to the school, along with the sixty-five cents left to be expended for the help of the school. That, it seemed to me, was another case of grasping the shadow instead of the substance. The engrossed resolutions were the shadow; the sixty-five cents were all that was left of the substance.

In all these matters we need speedy and effective reforms. We want you to go out into the world and use your influence toward securing these reforms. There are too many people in the world who give their whole lives to grasping at the shadow instead of the substance— grasping at a sham instead of real worth. We want you to teach by word and action simple, right and honest living.

Character as Shown in Dress

It is surprising how much we can tell about a person's character by his dress. I think it is very seldom that we cannot tell whether a person is ignorant or educated, simply by his dress; and there are some few, plain facts about dress that I am going to mention to you to-night. While it is hard to lay down any rules as to how we must dress, I think there are some well-defined principles of dress to which all well-educated persons will conform.

I think we will all agree that our dress should be clean. There is little excuse for persons wearing filthy clothes—I think we all will agree as to that. It is disgraceful for a man to go about with ragged clothes or with clothes fastened together with pins where buttons ought to be. It is disgraceful for a girl to go about with a soiled apron, or with her clothes pinned together. Our clothes should be kept clean and in good repair. Thus far, I think, we shall have no disagreement.

But there are some people who make the mistake of giving their whole mind to the subject of dress. From the very beginning of the week you will find that a great part of their thought and attention is given to planning what they are going to wear the next Sunday. Some people will go in rags all through the week, in order to have something showy to wear on Sunday. I think we should respect Sunday by putting on something different from what we wear during the week if we can—although of course these things are largely governed by our station in life—but even then it certainly is inappropriate to wear our most showy clothes on that day.

Dress in the way that your pocket will allow. There are some persons who not only employ all their thoughts in considering what they shall wear, but also spend all their money on their clothes.

There are some persons who live for the sake of dress. These persons are usually denominated "fops." I think the people in the Northern cities are the worst in this respect. If you go through Sixth Avenue, in New York, or Cambridge Street, in Boston, you will see many of these fops, who perhaps earn about twenty dollars a month, standing on the street corners with kid gloves on, cigars between their lips, and high hats. Now that kind of a person is a foolish fop, and one whom we do not care to have in this institution. There is no more foolish person than the one who spends all he makes, and sometimes more, on dress.

Then, too, I think there are persons who make mistakes in the matter of ornaments—what we call jewellery. You will find many a man whose income is not twenty dollars a month wearing a great brass watch chain with so much brass in it that you can almost smell it. You will see men and women with three or four brass finger rings, or women with brass ear-rings. Do you know that one of the most common mistakes among the masses of our people in the country is throwing away their money on cheap jewellery? Do you know that they will come in to town to the stores, and spend their money on jewellery worth about ten cents apiece, jewellery that you actually can get for six dollars and seven dollars a bushel at wholesale? Our people spend thousands of dollars every year for this cheap jewellery. If there is a young man or a young woman here who likes jewellery, and is going to indulge in it, be sure to get that which is modest.

Another mistake that some of our people make is in wearing flashy or loud dress—dress in which bright colours and red ribbons predominate. Our dress should be modest; with few colours.

We often make a mistake in getting shoes about two sizes too small. I saw a girl this morning in perfect misery, simply because she had bought, and was trying to wear, a pair of shoes about two sizes too small. Such people simply punish their feet to make people think they have small feet, though it is just as honourable to have a large foot as a small one; there is no difference. Then we make another mistake in buying cheap, showy shoes simply because they have a gloss on them. Such shoes are made to attract attention, and not for comfort or durability. When you are spending your money for shoes, be sure that you get something good, something that will last you. Do not buy those worthless things, which, when they come in contact with water, will shrivel up because they are made of cheap material. A man cannot respect a girl who punishes her feet in order to make them look small.

Then, another thing. Some of us think we can improve our colour. Some get flour, and others get other kinds of mixtures which are called face powders. There is no use for this. Any man will lose respect for a girl who abuses herself in this way. Only get something into your head, and then you will find that these matters of dress will adjust themselves. While some of you do not dress so well as you might, yet, if you will give the contents of your heads the proper attention, you will find that the matter of dress will not trouble you. You can get dresses and clothes after you have secured your education, but now is the only time that you have in which to secure the education.

BOOKER T. WASHINGTON

Sing the Old Songs

There is no part of our chapel exercises that gives me more pleasure than the beautiful Negro melodies which you sing. I believe there is no part of the service more truly spiritual, more elevating. Wherever you go, after you leave this school, I hope that you will never give up the singing of these songs. If you go out to have schools of your own, have your pupils sing them as you have sung them here, and teach them to see the beauty which dwells in these songs. When in New York, not long ago, I had the pleasure of conversing with Prince Henry of Prussia, he spoke particularly of the beauty of these songs, and said that in his own home, in Germany, he and his family often sing them. He asked if there was any printed collection of these songs, that a copy might be sent him, and I have since then forwarded to him a copy of the book of plantation melodies collected and published under the auspices of Hampton Institute.

When Christ was upon this earth He said: "A little child shall lead them." Whence comes this supreme power of leadership? In this age, when we hear so much said about leaders of men, about successful leadership, we do well to stop to consider this admonition of the Saviour. Some are said to lead in business, others in education, others in politics, or in religion. What is the explanation of "A little child shall lead them?" Simply this. A little child, under all circumstances, is its simple, pure, sweet self; never appearing big when it is little; never appearing learned when it is ignorant; never appearing wealthy when it is in poverty; never appearing important when it is unimportant. In a word, the life of the child is founded upon the great and immutable, and yet simple, tender and delicate laws of nature. There is no pretence. There is no mockery.

There is an unconscious, beautiful, strong clinging to truth; and it is this divine quality in child or in man, in Jew or Gentile, in Christian or Mohammedan, in the ancient world or in the modern world, in a black man or in a white man, that always has led men and moulded their activity. The men who have been brave enough, wise enough, simple enough, self-denying enough to plant themselves upon this rock of truth and there stand, have, in the end, drawn the world unto them, even as Christ said: "I will draw all men unto me." Such a man was Luther, such a man was Wesley, such a man was Carlyle, such a man was Cromwell, such were Garrison and Phillips, such was Abraham Lincoln, and such was our own great Frederick Douglass.

The thing aimed at by all great souls has been to bring men and races back to the simplicity and purity of childhood—back to reality.

What is the most original product with which the Negro race stands accredited? Yes, I am almost ready to add, with which America stands accredited? Without hesitation I answer:—Those beautiful, weird, quaint, sweet melodies which were the simple, child-like expression of the anguish, the joy, the hopes, the burdens, the faith, the trials of our forefathers who wore the yoke of slavery.

Why are they the admiration of the world? Why does every attempt at improvement spoil them? Why do they never fail to touch the tenderest chord—to bring tears from the eyes of rich and poor—from king and humblest toiler alike?

Listen how in this beautiful song the soul in trouble is told not to go to houses and temples made by man, but to get close to Nature:

Ef yer want to see Jesus
Go in de wilderness,
Go in de wilderness,
Go in de wilderness,
Go in de wilderness.
If yer want to see Jesus,
Go in de wilderness
Leanin' on de Lord.
Oh brudder, how d'ye feel, when ye come out de wilderness,
Come out de wilderness,
Come out de wilderness,
Oh, brudder, how d'ye feel, when ye come out de wilderness,
Leanin' on de Lord?

Then, in another, hear how our foreparents broke through all the deceptions and allurements of false wealth, and in their long days of weariness expressed their faith in a place where every day would be one of rest:

Oh, religion is a fortune,
I r'a'ly do believe.
Oh, religion is a fortune,
I r'a'ly do believe.

Oh, religion is a fortune,
I r'a'ly do believe,
Whar Sabbaths hab no end.
Whar yo' been, poor mourner, whar yo' been so long?
"Been down in de valley, for to pray;
An' I ain't done prayin' yet."

Then, how, when oppressed by years of servitude to which others thought there would be no end, we hear them break out into quaint and wild bursts of appeal to fact:

My Lord delibered Daniel,
My Lord delibered Daniel,
My Lord delibered Daniel;
Why can't He deliber me?
I met a pilgrim on de way, an' I ask him where he's gwine.
"I'm bound for Canaan's happy lan',
An' dis is de shoutin' band.
Go on."

He delibered Daniel from de lion's den,
Jonah from de belly ob de whale,
An' de Hebrew children from de fiery furnace.
Den why not ebery man?"

Or when the burden seemed almost too great for human body to endure, there came this simple, child-like prayer:

O Lord, O, my Lord, O, my good Lord,
Keep me from sinkin' down.
O Lord, O my Lord, O my good Lord,
Keep me from sinkin' down.
I tell yo' what I mean to do.
Keep me from sinkin' down.
I mean to go to hebben, too.
Keep me from sinkin' down.

Or what could go more directly to Nature's heart than the pathetic yet hopeful, trustful outburst of the little slave boy who was to be taken from his mother to be sold into the far South, when it seemed to him that all earthly happiness was forever blighted. Hear him:

I'm gwine to jine de great 'sociation,
I'm gwine to jine de great 'sociation,
I'm gwine to jine de great 'sociation.
Den my little soul's gwine to shine, shine;
Den my little soul's gwine to shine along. Oh!

I'm gwine to climb up Jacob's ladder.
Den my little soul's gwine to shine, shine.
Den my little soul's gwine to shine along. Oh!

I'm gwine to climb up higher an' higher.
Den my little soul's gwine, etc

I'm gwine to sit at de welcome table
I'm gwine to feast off milk an' honey.

I'm gwine to tell God how-a' you sarved me.
Den my little soul's gwine to shine, shine.
Den my little soul's gwine to shine along. Oh!

And so it has ever been, so it is, and ever will be. The world, regardless of race, or colour, or condition, admires and approves a real thing. But sham, buffoonery, mere imitation, mere superficiality, never has brought success and never will bring it.

An individual or a race that is strong enough, is wise enough, to disregard makeshifts, customs, prejudices, alluring temptations, deceptions, imitations—to throw off the mask of unreality and plant itself deep down in the clay, or on the solid granite of nature, is the individual or the race that will crawl up, struggle up, yes, even burst up; and in the effort of doing so will gain a strength that will command for it respect and recognition. Before an individual or a race thus equipped, race prejudice, senseless customs, oppressions, will hide their faces forever in blushing shame.

Getting Down to Mother Earth

One of the highest ambitions of every man leaving Tuskegee Institute should be to help the people of his race find bottom—find bed rock—and then help them to stand upon that foundation. If we who are interested in the school can help you to do this, we shall count ourselves satisfied. And until the bed-rock of our life is found, and until we are planted thereon, all else is but plaster, but make-believe, but the paper on the walls of a house without framework.

That is one of the stepping stones with which nature has provided us. Here the path is plain, if we have the courage to follow it. Eighty-five per cent. of the people of the Negro race live—or attempt to live—by some form of agriculture. If we would save the race, and lift it up, here is the great opportunity around which, in a large measure, individual, organized, religious and secular effort should centre for the next fifty years.

But to do this we must take advantage of the forces at hand. We must stand upon our own feet, and not upon a foundation supplied by another. We must begin our growth where our civilization finds us, and not try to begin on some other civilization.

To illustrate what I mean, we need not go to another race, nor very far from home. In a little town in Alabama there was a sturdy, industrious black man who for nearly twenty years had lived upon rented land, had hired mules and horses to work that land, and had mortgaged his crops to secure food and clothes. He had driven to church on Sunday in a buggy that was not his, and he wore good-looking clothes that were not paid for. In outward appearance he seemed to prosper. He seemed to be what the white men about him were.

But this black man knew that he was trying to stand upon an imperfect basis. And so, one day about a dozen years ago, he made up his mind that henceforth he would be himself—that he would stand upon his own foundation. He told the white man to take back his mules, to take back his waggon and buggy; and he gave up the rented land. He had resolved to be a man. A few acres of land were secured. He made his bed in the cotton seed at night. He hired a boy to come to his place at night, and by moonlight he pulled a plough which the boy guided. In this way a cotton crop was made free from debt. With the small surplus which he got from this he bought an ox, and with this beast made a second crop free from debt. A mule was bought, and then another. To-day this man is the owner of a comfortable home, is a stockholder in one of the banks of his county, and his note or check will be honoured by any business house there. While others were talking, or debating over second-hand doctrines learned by rote, this strong son of nature had found himself and solved his own problem.

I might tell you the story of another man of our race who began his successful business life in the hollow of a tree for his home; without furniture or bed-clothing. But that tree, and the land on which it stood, were his own. You had better begin life in a hollow tree and be a man, than begin it in a rented house and be a mere tool, the imitation of a man. If you were to go into the Western part of this country you would find it filled with men of the highest culture, profound scholarship, and enduring wealth, whose ancestors a few generations ago began life in a dug-out, in a hay loft, or in a hole in the side of a mountain. Young men and young women, there is no escape. If we would be great, and good, and useful, we must pay the price. And remember that when we get down to the fundamental principles of truth, nature draws no colour line.

I do not want to startle you when I say it, but I should like to see during the next fifty years every coloured minister and teacher, whose work lies outside the large cities, armed with a thorough knowledge of theoretical and practical agriculture, in connection with his theological and academic training. This, I believe, should be so because the race is an agricultural one, and because my hope is that it will remain such. Upon this foundation almost every race in history has got its start. With cheap lands, a beautiful climate and a rich soil, we can lay the foundation of a great and powerful race. The question that confronts us is whether we will take advantage of this opportunity?

In a recent number of the New York *Independent*, Rev. Russel H. Conwell, the pastor of the great Temple Baptist Church, in Philadelphia, a church that has a membership of three thousand persons, tells of the pastor of a small country church in Massachusetts who, in perplexity at the eternally recurring question of how to make his church pay its expenses, asked Mr. Conwell's advice. "I advised him," Mr. Conwell says, "to study agricultural chemistry, dairy farming and household economy. I meant the advice seriously, and he took it seriously. He made his studies, and he made them thoroughly. On the Sunday when he preached his first practical sermon which was the outgrowth of his helpful learning, its topic was scientific manures, with appropriate scriptural allusions.

He had just seventeen listeners. These seventeen, however, were greatly interested. Later on, they discussed the remarkable departure with their friends who had not attended the service. The result was that within five Sundays the church was packed with worshippers, who had discovered that heaven is not such a long distance from earth after all."

In the present condition of our race, what an immense gain it would be if from every church in the vast agricultural region of the South there could be preached every Sunday two sermons on religion, and a lesson or lecture given on the principles of intelligent agriculture, on the importance of the ownership of land, and on the importance of building comfortable homes. I believe that if this policy could be pursued, instead of the now too often poorly clothed, poorly fed, and poorly housed ministers, with salaries ranging from one hundred to three hundred dollars a year, we should soon have communities and churches on their feet, to such an extent that hundreds of ministers who now live at a dying rate would be supported in a manner commensurate with the dignity of the profession. Not only this, but such a policy would result in giving the ministry such an ideal of the dignity of labour and such a love for it, that the minister's own home and garden and farm would be constant object lessons for his followers, and at the same time sources from which he could draw a support which would make him in a large measure independent.

One of the most successful and most honoured ministers I know is a man who owns and cultivates fifty acres of land. This land yields him an income sufficient to live on each year. This man's note or check is gladly honoured at the bank. Because of his independence he leads his people instead of having to cater to their whims. It may be suggested that what I plead for has not been done by others, after this fashion. It was done in the early years of the settlement of New England, and persevered in by the ministers there until the people of the country had become sufficiently prosperous to support their ministers suitably. Besides, if one race of people, or one individual, is simply to follow in the steps of another, no progress would ever be possible in the world. Let us remember that no other race of people ever had just such a problem to work out as we have.

What I have tried to say to you to-night about agricultural life may be said with equal emphasis about city occupations. Show me the race that leads in work in wood and in metal, in the building of houses and factories, and in the constructing and operating of machinery, and I will show you the race that in the long run moulds public thought, that controls government, that leads in commerce, in the sciences, in the arts and in the professions.

What we should do in all our schools is to turn out fewer job-seekers and more job-makers. Any one can seek a job, but it requires a person of rare ability to create a job.

If it may seem to some of you that what I have been saying overlooks the development of the race in morals, ethics, religion and statesmanship, my answer would be this. You might as well argue that because a tree is planted deep down in Mother Earth, because it comes in contact with clay, and rocks, and sand, and water, that through its graceful branches, its beautiful leaves and its fragrant blossoms it teaches no lesson of truth, beauty and divinity. You cannot plant a tree in air and have it live. Try it. No matter how much we may praise its proportions and enjoy its beauty, it dies unless its roots and fibres touch and have their foundation in Mother Earth. What is true of the tree is true of a race.

A Penny Saved

A large proportion of you, for one reason or another, will not be able to return to this institution after the close of the present year. On that account there are some central thoughts which I should like to impress upon your minds this evening, and which I wish you to take with you into the world, whether you go out from the school as graduates or whether you go as undergraduates.

I have often spoken to you about the matter of learning to economize your time, to save your time, the matter of trying to make the most of every minute and hour of your existence. I have often spoken to you about the hurtful reputation which a large proportion of the people of our race get in one way or another because of this seeming inability to put a proper value upon time, or a proper value upon the importance of keeping one's word in connection with obligations.

You know to what a large extent the feeling prevails—whether justly or unjustly—that as a people we cannot be depended upon to keep our word; that if we are hired to work in a mill or a factory, we work until we have got three dollars or four dollars in wages ahead, and then go on an excursion, or go to town, and do not return to work until what we have earned has been consumed.

And so, in one way or another, a large proportion of us get the reputation that we cannot be depended upon for faithful, regular, efficient service; and that hurts the race. Wherever you go, we wish you by your own actions, by your advice, by your influence, to try and disprove and counteract that hurtful reputation. You can do this in the most efficient manner by yourselves being the highest possible example.

The people who succeed are, very largely, those who learn to economize time, in the ways I have referred to, and those who also have learned to save, not only time, but money.

Now this may seem to you a very materialistic thought for me to emphasize this evening—the saving of money—but to us, as a race, it is of vital importance. I have heard it expressed recently on several occasions that the Negro was becoming too much materialized, too much industrialized. Too much attention, it has been said, is given to the material side of life. Now it seems to me that I have as yet seen very little that need arouse our fears in that direction. I am not able to understand how a race that does not own a single steam railroad, that does not own a single street-car line, that owns hardly a bank, that does not own a single block of houses in a large city—I am not able to understand how such a race as that is in danger of becoming materialized. When you get millions of dollars in banks, when you get millions of dollars invested in railroad stocks, when you get other millions invested in street-car lines, or in the control of large factories, great plantations, or in other great industrial enterprises in the South, then I shall say that there are signs of your becoming too materialistic, of your getting to be too rich; but I do not see any such signs yet. And until we do see such signs, we can rest ourselves in peace, I think, so far as that danger is concerned.

But there is a certain influence of money that I do not think we emphasize enough. In the first place the getting hold of money, the getting hold of a competency, insures us the possession of certain influences that we can get in no other way. In order to get hold of the spiritually best and highest things in life there are certain material things that we are compelled to have first. In the first place the getting hold of money and the saving of this money will assure the possession of decent comfortable houses to live in. No person can do his best work, or can be of the greatest service to himself and to his fellow-beings, until he is able to live in a decent, comfortable house. You will not be ready for life until you own such a house, whether you live in it or not. Even if you own such a house and rent it out, you are that much more of a man. I often hear people say that they do not own a house, or property, because they do not expect to live long in this place or that place. I have known such people to move six times in six years. They never will own a house, simply because they have got into the habit of giving excuses, instead of trying to get to own a home.

The possession of a decent house insures us a certain amount of proper comfort. No person can do the best work, can think well, can get along well, unless he has a certain amount of comfort, and, I may add, a certain amount of good, nourishing food, well cooked. The person who is not sure where he is going to get his breakfast, or the one who is not sure where he is going to get the money to pay his next week's board, is the individual who cannot do the best work, whether the work be physical, mental or spiritual. The possession of money enables us to be sure that we are going to have comfortable clothing, clothing enough to keep the body warm and vigorous, and in good, healthy condition.

BOOKER T. WASHINGTON

The possession of money enables us to get to the point where we can do our part in the building of school-houses, churches, hospitals; it enables us to do our part in all these directions. Money not only enables us to get upon our feet in these material directions, but it has another value. The getting of it develops foresight on our part. People cannot get money without learning to exercise forethought, without planning to-day for to-morrow, this week for the next week, and this year for next year. People cannot get hold of money—or at least cannot keep hold of it—who have not learned to exercise self-control. They must be able to say "No." I want you students, when you go out from here, to be able to say "No." I want you to be able to go by a store and, as you notice the things in that store—whether candy or spring hats, or whatever it is that attracts you—to be able, notwithstanding the fact that you have the money in your pockets to buy, to exercise a self-control that will enable you to pass these things by and save your money to invest it in a home. Persons cannot get hold of money without learning to exercise economy, without learning to make everything go just as far as it is possible to make it go.

Then, again, the getting money enables a person to become a good, steady, safe citizen. The people who kill and are killed, nine times out of ten, whether they are black or white, are people who do not own a home, who do not have money in the bank. They are people who live in their gripsacks. They are gripsack leaders. If their gripsacks are in Montgomery to-night, there is their home. If they are in Opelika the next night, there is their home that night. There are numbers of these people who have no home except their gripsacks. Now I don't want you to go out from here to be that kind of men and women. I want to see you own land. I want to see you own a decent home. And let me say right here that your home is not decent or complete unless it contains a good, comfortable bath-tub. Of the two, I believe I would rather see you own a bathtub without a house, than a house without a bathtub. If you get the tub you are sure to get the house later. So when you go out from here, buy a bathtub, even if you cannot afford to buy anything else.

The possession of money, the having of a bank account, even if small, gives us a certain amount of self-respect. An individual who has a bank account walks through a street so much more erect; he looks people in the face. The people in the community in which he lives have a confidence in him and a respect for him which they would not have if he did not possess the bank account.

Now one great mistake that we make in striving to reach these things is that we keep putting off beginning. The young man says that he will begin when he gets married. The young woman says that she will begin when she gets dressed well enough, or gets a little further on in life. Yielding to this temptation or to that, they keep putting off beginning to save. It makes one sick at heart, as he goes into the cities, to see young men on Sunday afternoons paying two or three dollars for a hack or carriage to take young women out to drive, when in too many cases the men do not earn a salary of more than four dollars a week. Young women, don't go driving with such men. A man who goes driving on a salary of four dollars a week cannot own a home or possess a bank account. When you are asked to go to drive by such a man as that, tell him you would rather he would put his money in the bank, because you know he is not able to afford to spend it in that way.

I like to see people comfortably and neatly dressed; but there is no sadder sight than to see young men and women yielding to the temptation to spend all they earn upon clothes. Then when they die—in many, many cases—somebody has to pass around a hat to take up a collection in order that they may be decently put away. Do not make that mistake. Resolve that no matter how little you may earn, you will put a part of the money in the bank. If you earn five dollars a week, put two dollars in the bank. If you earn ten dollars, save four of them. Put the money in the bank. Let it stay there. When it begins to draw interest you will find that you will appreciate the value of money.

A little while ago I was in the city of New Bedford, the city which was formerly the home of Mrs. Hetty Green, who is said to be the richest woman in the world. I want to tell you a story about her that was told me by a gentleman who lived in New Bedford, and who knew Mrs. Green when she lived there. For many years they had in New Bedford no savings bank that would take a very small deposit. Finally a five-cent savings bank was opened there. Just after this had been done, Mrs. Green told this gentleman that she was glad they had opened a five-cent bank, so that now she would be able to put that amount in and have it draw interest. You who are here do not think about five cents as a sum to be saved. You think of it only as money to buy peanuts and candy, or cheap ribbons, or cheap jewellery.

On last Sunday evening I was in the home of a gentleman in New York who has in his family a girl who is now only eighteen years old, and who, when she came to this country a few years ago and went to work in this family as a maid, could not speak a word of English. This girl now has fifteen hundred dollars in the bank. Think of it! A young woman coming to this country poor, and unable to speak a word of English, has saved in a short time fifteen hundred dollars! I wonder how many of you, five years from now, will have fifteen hundred dollars in the bank or in some other safe kind of property.

The civilization of New England and of other such prosperous regions rests more, perhaps, upon the savings banks of the country than upon any other one thing. You ask where the wealth of New England is. It is not in the hands of millionaires. It is in the hands of individuals, who have a few hundreds or a few thousands of dollars put safely away in some bank or banks. You will find that the savings banks of New England, and of all countries that are prosperous, are filled with the dollars of poor people, dollars aggregating millions in all.

We cannot get upon our feet, as a people, until we learn the saving habit; until we learn to save every nickel, every dime and every dollar that we can spare.

GROWTH

I want to impress upon you this evening the importance of continued growth. I very much wish that each one of you might imagine, this evening, your father and your mother to be looking at you and examining into every act of your life while here. I wish that you might feel, as it were, their very heart throbs. I wish that you might realize, perhaps as you have never realized before, how anxious they are that you should succeed here. I wish that you could know how many prayers they send up, day after day, that your school life may be more and more successful as one day succeeds another, that you may grow to be successful, studious, strong men and women, who will reflect credit upon yourselves and honour upon your families.

Each one of you must have had some thoughts about those who are anxious about you, some thought for those persons whose hearts are very often bowed down in anxiety because they fear your school life here will not be successful. Not only for your own sake, but for the sake of those who are near and dear to you, those who have done more for you than anybody else, I want you to make up your minds that this year is going to be the best one of your lives.

I want you to resolve that you are going to put into this year the hardest and the most earnest work that you have ever done in your life, to resolve that this is going to be the greatest, the most courageous and the most sinless year of life that you have ever lived; I want you to make up your minds to do this; to decide that you are going to continually grow—and grow more to-morrow than to-day. There are but two directions in this life in which you can grow; backward or forward. You can grow stronger, or you can grow weaker; you can grow greater, or smaller; but it will be impossible for you to stand still.

Now in regard to your studies; your lessons. I want you to make up your minds that you are going to be more and more thorough in your lessons each day you remain here; that you are going to so discipline yourselves that each morning will find you in the recitation rooms with your lessons more thoroughly and more conscientiously prepared for the day's work than they were for the work of the day before. I want you to make up your minds that you are going to be more nearly perfect, are going to put more manly and womanly strength into the preparation of your lessons each day, that you may be more useful. Then you will find yourselves wanting to grow, I hope; will find yourselves learning the dignity of labour, and that no class of people can get up and stay up, can be strong and useful and respected, until they learn that there is no disgrace in any form of labour.

I hope you are learning that labour with the hand, in any form whatever, is not disgraceful. I hope that you are learning, day by day, that all kinds of labour—whether with the mind or with the hand—are honourable, and that people only disgrace themselves by being and keeping in idleness.

I want you to go forward by thoroughness in your work; by being more conscientious in your work; by loving your work more to-day than you did yesterday. If you are not growing in these respects—that is, if you are not going forward—you are going backward, and are not answering the purpose for which this institution was established, are not answering the purpose for which your parents sent you here.

I want to emphasize the fact that we want you to grow in the direction of character—to grow stronger each day in the matter of character. When I say character, here, I mean to use the word in its broadest sense. The institution wants to find you growing more polite to your fellows every day, as you come in contact with them, whether it be in the class-room, in the shop, in the field, in the dining-room, or in your bedroom. No matter where you are, I want you to find yourselves growing more polite and gentlemanly. Notice I do not say merely that I want your teachers—those who are over you—to find you growing more polite; I want you to find yourselves so. If you are not doing this, you are going backward, you are going in the wrong direction.

I want to find you each day more thoughtful of others, and less selfish. I want you to be more conscientious in your thoughts and in your work, and with regard to your duty toward others. This is growing in the right direction; not doing this is growing in the wrong direction. Nor do I want you to feel that you are to strive for this spirit of growth for this one year alone, or for the time that you are here. I hope that you will continue to grow in the forward direction.

Then, and this is more important still, we want you to take this habit of growth—this disposition to grow in the right direction—out with you from the school, and scatter it as an influence for good wherever you go. We want you to take it into your schools; for many of you are going to become teachers. We want you not only to begin it when you begin teaching in an humble way, but we want to see you grow and improve in it every year. We want to see you make your school-houses more attractive; to see you make everything in connection with your schools and your teaching better and stronger; to see you make a school more useful every year that you remain as its teacher.

Then, too, when you go out and get employment—no matter of what kind it may be—we want to see you grow better in that employment; we want to see you advance in ability, commanding always a larger salary, advancing in value to those who employ you. We want to see you grow in reputation for being honest, conscientious, intelligent, hard-working; no matter in what capacity you are employed.

Some of you are going out to establish homes and settle down in home life. We want to see you grow in that direction. Nothing is so disheartening—there is nothing so discouraging—as to see a man or woman settle down in a home, and then not to see that home grow more beautiful, inside and outside;—to see it, instead of this, each year grow dingy and dirty, because it each year receives less and less attention.

We want Tuskegee students to go out from here and establish homes that will be models in every respect for those about them—homes that will show that the lives of the persons who have established them are models for the lives of those who live about them. If you do this, your lives are going to be a constant going forward; for, I repeat, your lives are going to be one thing or the other, continually going backward or continually going forward.

Last Words

We have come to the close of another school year. Some of you will go out from among us now, not to return. Others will go home for the summer vacation and return at the end of that for the next school year.

As you go out, there is one thing that I want to especially caution you about. Don't go home and feel that you are better than the rest of the folks in your neighbourhood because you have been away at school. Don't go home and feel ashamed of your parents because you think they don't know as much as you think you know. Don't think that you are too good to help them. It would be better for you not to have any education, than for you to go home and feel ashamed of your parents, or not want to help them.

Let me tell you of one of the most encouraging and most helpful things that I have known of in connection with the life of our students after they leave this institution. I was in a Southern city, and going about among the homes of the people of our race. Among these homes I noticed one which was so neat looking that it was conspicuous. I asked the person who was with me, "How is it that this house is in such good condition, looks so much better than some of the others in the neighbourhood?" "It is like this," said the man who was accompanying me. "The people who live there have a son whom they sent to your school, at considerable self-denial to themselves. This young man came home from school a few weeks ago. For some time after he came back he did not have work to keep him busy, and so he employed his spare time in fixing up his parents' home. He fixed the roof and chimney, put new palings in the fence where they were needed and did such things as that. Then he got a stock of paint and painted the house thoroughly, two coats, outside and in. That is why the place looks so neat."

Such testimony as that is very helpful. It shows that the students carry out from here the spirit which we try to inculcate.

Another thing. Go home and lead a simple life. Don't give the impression that you think education means superficiality and dress.

Be polite; to white and coloured people, both. It is possible for you, by paying heed to this, to do a great deal toward securing and preserving pleasant relations between the people of both races in the South. Try to have your manners in this respect so good that people will notice them and ask where you have been, at what school you learned to be so polite. You will find that politeness counts for a great deal, not only in helping you to get work, but in helping you to keep it.

Don't be ashamed to go to church and Sunday school, to the Young Men's Christian Association and the Christian Endeavour Society. Show that education has only deepened your interest in such things. Have no going backward. Be clean, in your person, your language and in your thoughts.

It seems appropriate during these closing days of the school year to re-emphasize, if possible, that for which the institution stands. We want to have every student get what we have—in our egotism, perhaps—called the "Tuskegee spirit"; that is, to get hold of the spirit of the institution, get hold of that for which it stands; and then spread that spirit just as widely as possible, and plant it just as deeply as it is possible to plant it.

In addition to the members of our graduating class, we have each year a large number of students who go out to spend their vacations. Some of these will return at the close of vacation, but some, for various reasons, will not return. Whether you go out as graduates, whether you go out to return or not to return, it is important that all of you get hold of the "Tuskegee spirit"; the spirit of giving yourselves, in order that you may help lift up others. In no matter how small a degree it may be, see that you are assisting some one else.

Now, after a number of years' experience, the institution feels that it has reached a point where it can, with some degree of authority, give advice as to the best way in which you can spend your life.

In the first place, as to your location—the place where you shall work. I very much hope that the larger part of the students who go out from Tuskegee will choose the country districts for their place of work, rather than the large cities. For one thing, you will find that the larger places are much better supplied with workers and helpers than is true of the towns, and especially of the country districts. The cities are better supplied with churches and schools, with everything that tends to uplift people; and they are at the same time much more prolific of those agencies which tend to pull people down. Notwithstanding this latter fact, the greater portion, by far, of those who need help live in the country districts. I think a census report will show that eighty per cent. of our people are to be found in the country and small towns. I advise you, then, to go into the country and the towns, rather than into the cities.

BOOKER T. WASHINGTON

Then, as to the manner of work. You must make up your minds in the first place, as I have said before, that you are going to make some sacrifice, that you are going to live your lives in an unselfish way, in order that you may help some one. Go out with a spirit that will not allow you to become discouraged when you have opposition, when you meet with obstacles to be overcome. You must go with a determination that you are going to succeed in whatever undertaking you have entered upon.

I do not attempt to give you specific advice as to the kind of work you shall do, but I should say that in a general way I believe that you can accomplish more good—and perhaps this will hold good for the next fifty years here in the South—by taking a country school for your nucleus. Take a three months school, and gradually impress upon the people of the community the need of having a longer school. Get them to add one month to three months, and then another month, until they get to the point where they will have six, seven or eight months of school in a year. Then get them to where they will see the importance of building a decent school-house—getting out of the one-room log cabin school-house—and of having suitable apparatus for instruction.

There are two things you must fix your mind on: the building of a suitable school-house and the arousing in the people, at the same time, a spirit that will make them support your efforts. In order to do this you must go into the country with the idea of staying there for some time at least. Plant yourself in the community, and by economical living, year by year, manage to buy land for yourself, on which to build a nice and comfortable home. You will find that the longer you stay there the more the people will give you their confidence, and the more they will respect and love you.

I find that many of our graduates have done excellent work by having a farm in connection with their schools. This is true, also, of many who did not remain here to graduate. I have in mind such a man. He has been teaching school in one of the counties of this State for seven or eight years. He has lengthened the school year to eight months. He has a nice cottage with four rooms in it, and a beautiful farm of forty acres. This man is carrying out the "Tuskegee idea."

There will be some of you who can spend your life to better advantage by devoting it to farming than to any other industry. I speak of farming particularly, because I believe that to be the great foundation upon which we must build for the future. I believe that we are coming to the point where we are going to be recognized for our worth in the proportion that we secure an agricultural foundation. Throughout the South we can give ourselves in a free, open way to getting hold of property and building homes, in a way that we cannot do in any other industry. In farming, as in teaching, no matter where you go, remember to go with the "Tuskegee spirit."

I want the boys to go out and do as Mr. N. E. Henry is doing; I want the girls to go out and do as Miss Anna Davis and Miss Lizzie Wright are doing. I want you to go out into the country districts and build up schools. I would not advise you to be too ambitious at first. Be willing to begin with a small salary and work your way up gradually. I have in mind one young man who began teaching school for five dollars a month; another who began teaching in the open air under a tree.

Then, too, I want you to go out in a spirit of liberality toward the white people with whom you come in contact. That is an important matter. When I say this I do not mean that you shall go lowering your manhood or your dignity. Go in a manly way, in a straightforward and honourable way, and then you will show the white people that you are not of a belittling race, that the prejudice which so many people possess cannot come among you and those with whom you work. If you can extend a helping hand to a white person, feel just as happy in doing so as in helping a black person.

In the sight of God there is no colour line, and we want to cultivate a spirit that will make us forget that there is such a line anywhere. We want to be larger and broader than the people who would oppress us on account of our colour.

No one ever loses anything by being a gentleman or a lady. No person ever lost anything by being broad. Remember that if we are kind and useful, if we are moral, if we go out and practise these traits, no matter what people say about us, they cannot pull us down. But, on the other hand, if we are without the spirit of usefulness, if we are without morality, without liberality, without economy and property, without all those qualities which go to make a people and a nation great and strong, no matter what we may say about ourselves and what other people may say about us, we are losing ground. Nobody can give us those qualities merely by praising us and talking well about us; and when we possess them, nobody can take them from us by speaking ill of us.

A Note About the Author

Booker T. Washington (1856–1915) was a prominent figure in the African American community and a champion of higher education. He was born into slavery and obtained freedom shortly after the Emancipation Proclamation. As a child, he worked manual jobs to help support his family, but aspired to receive a formal education. He enrolled in Hampton Normal Agricultural Institute in Virginia and thrived as a student. After graduating, Washington embarked on a career as a lecturer and leader of the Tuskegee Institute. He also worked as a political advisor to presidents Theodore Roosevelt and William Taft.

A Note from the Publisher

Spanning many genres, from non-fiction essays to literature classics to children's books and lyric poetry, Mint Edition books showcase the master works of our time in a modern new package. The text is freshly typeset, is clean and easy to read, and features a new note about the author in each volume. Many books also include exclusive new introductory material. Every book boasts a striking new cover, which makes it as appropriate for collecting as it is for gift giving. Mint Edition books are only printed when a reader orders them, so natural resources are not wasted. We're proud that our books are never manufactured in excess and exist only in the exact quantity they need to be read and enjoyed.

bookfinity™

Discover more of your favorite classics with Bookfinity™.

- Track your reading with custom book lists.
- Get great book recommendations for your personalized Reader Type.
- Add reviews for your favorite books.
- AND MUCH MORE!

Visit **bookfinity.com** and take the fun Reader Type quiz to get started.

Enjoy our classic and modern companion pairings!

 Classic & Modern